The Anatomy of Success

Nicolas Darvas

Contents

If this life be not a real fight, in which something is eternally gained for the universe by success, it is no better than a game of private theatricals from which one may withdraw at will. But it feels like a real fight.

—William James

The Anatomy of Success

Introduction

SOME FRIENDS OF MINE ONCE CAME TO ME AND ASKED IF I would spend an hour or so with an acquaintance of theirs—a European who had been in the United States for close to seven years and was, as they described him, "entirely lost." Now in his early forties, this man was convinced he had made nothing of his life and was headed in an even more aimless direction than the one which he had been following. In the short time he had been in this country, he had had a series of low-paying and otherwise unfulfilling jobs. But something in the dim reaches of his soul told him that he should be successful at *something*. Exactly what it was he had talent for, however, he had no idea. My friends asked me to see him and give him some advice.

When this man and I met for the first time, there were

two things that impressed me immediately: the first was that
he was dressed with impeccable elegance which pointed to
excellent taste; and the second was that he had a marvellous
speaking voice which created an impression of extraordinary
sophistication. My initial reaction was extremely favourable,
and I was certain there would be many talents this stranger
would reveal to me before our meeting was at an end.

I was mistaken.

Aside from the generally amiable disposition he displayed, there was nothing especially shattering about either
his intelligence or his personality. For one thing, he seemed
almost incredibly naïve about matters related to what is
generally considered the business world. And for another,
he seemed totally devoid of creativity or imagination. He had
no special interests aside from trips to museums or reading
art columns in the newspapers. He was, in short, one of
those *seemingly* colourless individuals who, one is convinced,
could never in a thousand years build a career of any
significance for himself.

I was just at the point of cutting our meeting short,
extending my hand to him and—rather unhopefully, I'm
afraid—wishing him the best of luck when quite suddenly
the thought occurred to me: was I not being a trifle hasty in
dismissing this man as a "hopeless case"? Wasn't there *something* special about him? There had to be. I realized then
that I had nearly forgotten what most impressed me about
him at the beginning of our meeting.

I knew at that point that I was being hasty in trying to
shrug off this individual's career problems. There were, as
there are in the case of nearly everyone, distinguishing
characteristics. And in this man's case, they were what I've
already stated: he had excellent taste, and his speech, marked by a charming European accent, commanded one's in-

terest and attention. Why, then, couldn't this man capitalize on these very assets, despite the fact that they appeared comparatively minor when one considered his total personality?

The first suggestion which occurred to me took the form of a question. Had he ever considered the possibility of becoming a social secretary? Rarely have I seen a man so surprised. Did I consider being a social secretary the epitome of success, he asked? He only changed his expression when I pointed out that I only made this suggestion because it would lead to a promising area, an area where his elegant manner and his interest in the arts would be considered an asset. The area I thought of was in antiques. He did not answer me directly, but he did say he would think about it.

Several months passed. And a curious thing occurred. Not only did the man secure a job as a social secretary to a prominent New York family, but he liked the idea of selling antiques. Partially through the family's assistance, he proceeded to secure part-time, free-lance work as a representative to sell antique Italian furniture.

It hasn't taken this man long to acquire a fundamental knowledge of antiques, and through the contacts he has made in social circles, this seemingly "hopeless case" within a few years has become one of the best known antique dealers in the world with 27 offices in various countries.

The experience taught me an interesting lesson. It is simply this: the individual in search of success should consider every attribute he possesses, *no matter how minor this attribute may appear*. The person to whom I gave the advice is hardly a distinguished thinker. Nor would he prove particularly adept in a highly competitive business situation. But he—like everyone else—has assets. And he has made capital of them.

I have always been convinced that anyone can become an outstanding success, providing several factors are true: he has analysed himself thoroughly to know the field for which he is best suited; he has analysed the field itself and has decided on the path of least resistance to achieve the goal, and while moving towards it, has forever kept his eye on that goal, never wavering for one moment from the direction he was to follow, always building upon the very things most significant to making gains.

Achieving success is, essentially, a simple process. It follows in every case—no matter what the profession or career may be—a simple formula.

I myself have worked in many fields and, at the risk of sounding self-laudatory, I can honestly say I have been very successful. At one time, I became world famous as an acrobatic dancer. And during a subsequent period of my life, I made a name for myself, creating a brand-new image, as an author.

Later, I went on to explore and become successful in other fields—the fashion industry, theatrical producing, real estate are a few examples. Throughout these varied careers, a realization became very clear to me, particularly as each success piled upon the other.

The realization was this: no matter what the field, no matter what the area of life in which you hope to achieve your success, *the formula for success remains essentially the same.*

I began to see that there was no walk of life where a certain series of definite rules concerning success would not apply. And once I became aware of the rules, the solutions to problems were immeasurably simplified. But in order to achieve what one wanted, *the rules had to be followed.*

It was about the time I discovered this simple fact that I

became aware that there was such a thing as an "anatomy of success," an actual structural make-up which could be readily dissected. When I realized this, the thought suddenly occurred to me—why not dissect that anatomy myself for others to follow, letting them know exactly what steps to take, which directions to pursue and which to disregard? How much easier achieving and maintaining success might be if someone had the principles already set up and laid out in concise terms to follow! Not only would the individual be saving years of a painful try-and-fail procedure to achieve something (which in some cases he might not even want), but also he could use these precepts as guide-posts to his particular goal and even after he had already attained it.

Thus, I developed the idea of writing this book.

The conclusions I've made in the pages that follow are based on my own personal experiences and the experiences of many others I've known who were themselves involved to a great degree with success. Some of these individuals have spent years struggling desperately to unearth the right directions to follow, the moves to make, the proper feelings to help them make their decisions.

I am writing, then, what I and others have already learned. And one of the purposes I hope this book will fulfil is to save the reader valuable time, clarifying issues so that what might ordinarily be accomplished over a period of years could be successfully carried out in a period of months.

It was Goethe who said that in a world of confusion, a confused man only adds to the confusion. And it is time, as far as success is concerned, that this confusion be brought to an end.

Now, there are several points I should like to make before going into the direct steps you have to follow.

First of all, obtaining success is not a difficult or complex thing. And secondly, successful people are not especially mysterious. In most cases, what creates their success is that they know where they are going, they recognize what is important to their goals and have managed to disregard what isn't.

A man who is born rich may have some advantages over one who is born poor. But the poor man is like a horse with a handicap. He has a weight on him during the race, but he is still very much in the running. And if he's truly cut out for success, he will win.

It has been said that Napoleon's method of conquering a fortress was so simple it deluded everyone. While his enemies were trying to imagine the most complicated, roundabout methods Napoleon might be using to achieve a particular victory, he simply spotted his target and moved in a direct line towards it until it was conquered.

My book is divided into two sections: *Success: Achieving It* and *Success: Protecting It.* In the first section, I have boiled down the basic steps you have to follow to arrive at your goal; in the second section, I have stressed the importance of maintaining that goal and illustrated the various ways our successes might be affected by, among other things, money, marriage, sex, or the individual's personal reputation.

Once the steps are known and the correct rules followed, the rest is easy. Apply the facts in this book to your own particular situation, keeping your own particular personality traits, ambitions, and personal needs always in mind. Remember, success is not a vague, dreamlike thing, arrived at only by travelling a tangled, complicated pathway. Achieving and maintaining it are essentially simple.

But one must know the correct route.

Introduction

In a sense, then, let this book be your road map. Follow the guide-posts as they appear. Check off each destination after you've reached it. And keep it with you, continuing in the proper direction towards the fulfilment of your own particular dreams of glory.

N.D.

PART ONE

SUCCESS

Achieving It

1 Success: *What It Means*

ONE AFTERNOON ABOUT A YEAR AGO, I RECEIVED A TELE-
phone call from an old friend who had just made an
enormous killing on the stock market. He suggested we
meet for lunch to discuss his good fortune. I was delighted
with the idea, for I've always loved to hear stories about
people who become millionaires overnight.

My friend had been a reasonably well-to-do individual.
He had dabbled for years in the market. He'd made a little
money here and there, but he had not proved himself to
be what most people would consider a full-fledged success
in that area—that is, not until a month or so before I
received his phone call.

As I looked forward to our meeting, I tried to imagine
the subtle changes that might have taken place in my friend's
personality. For one thing, I was certain he would appear

enormously self-assured—a bit cocky, perhaps. I was sure, too, that he would be bubbling over with delight at his stroke of fortune.

You can imagine my astonishment when I found him waiting for me, crouched against the wall at one of the back tables of the restaurant, looking like a gaunt shadow of the man he had once been. In addition to being extremely nervous and withdrawn, he had developed the entirely unwholesome trait of *verbal self-flagellation.*

He kept telling me, of all things, how he really hadn't intended to make so much money. It had been mostly luck; he even made it sound as if it had been *bad* luck. He stressed the old cliché that money wasn't everything, that though he had achieved what he had always wanted in the business world, the achievement was essentially worthless.

At first, I was afraid that perhaps there was something the matter in my friend's personal life—perhaps his wife had fallen in love with another man; or maybe his children had become involved in some kind of serious trouble with the law. I asked him bluntly what was bothering him. But he merely laughed when I suggested that there was some problem in his personal life. He swore his family had never been happier. It seemed, at least, *they* were enjoying the money.

Then, I realized exactly what it was that was troubling him. He was suffering from the success syndrome in reverse. Instead of sitting back and enjoying what he had attained, he had become filled with guilt over it. It all seemed too easy, too comfortable. Something just had to be wrong—his anxiety told him so.

At the risk of sounding a little like his analyst, I tried to bring him around to some serious thinking on the subject of his success. Wasn't it true that he had spent many years working towards his particular goal of becoming a million-aire? Hadn't he already gone through enough anguish and sacrifice in his life in order to make his fortune? This was what he had been working for ever since he had graduated from college, and now that he had attained what he wanted, he could relax—or better still, set up another goal for himself which would carry him even farther.

Nearly everyone is familiar with the type of individual who flaunts his success all over the place. He may do it with a sparkling Rolls-Royce or he may do it with a stream of women whom he escorts nightly to El Morocco. Though the type of individual who *flaunts* his success is not exactly admirable, one thing should be quite clear: he is an in-finitely more healthy individual than the man who cringes in guilt from his own triumph.

Consider the facts. It is the rare individual who comes by success through a fluke. Success achieved in this manner seldom remains. Lasting success comes only through planning and execution. It comes from sheer hard work, the results of which should be enjoyed and respected, since it is directed towards receiving the fulfilment of one's inner-most dream.

In some quarters, success is peculiarly regarded as a four-letter word. William James spoke of success as "the bitch Goddess," which is altogether absurd when one con-siders that James himself was an enormous success in the areas of philosophy and psychology. Other people assert that success is nothing but sheer luck. This, again, is nonsense.

It takes talent—and will—to attain success. Luck is only a factor and a comparatively minor one.

A young actor happens to walk into a casting office at the exact moment when that office is looking for his particular type. He is luckier, let us say, than the young woman who walks into the same office and is looking for a job as a belly dancer. But what does the lucky actor do with that twist of fate once it comes his way? Does he give a good reading of the available role—or does his fortune of having been at "the right place at the right time" so throw him off guard that he nervously chokes his way through the scene?

Abe Burrows once described his version of luck on a nationwide TV show. Burrows said he saw luck as a wheel, with the lucky number coming his way at a particular time, then passing in a clockwise motion until it reached him once again at a subsequent time. The idea, of course, is to recognize at which time which of the numbers is the lucky one—and then reach out for it.

I know of a man who, in the 1930s, was given the chance to leave what he considered a dreary teaching job and accept an offer to go to work in a startling and promising new enterprise in San Francisco. But he didn't want to risk whatever financial security the teaching job had to offer and turned down the San Francisco spot. Some time later, this enterprise developed into an astonishing success for all those connected with it. The teacher had fumbled when the lucky number came his way.

Curiously enough, several years afterwards, the teacher, who was now even more embittered and unhappy in his job, was offered another opportunity that looked extremely promising. But by this time he had become so disgruntled, he overlooked any chance he might receive for the attainment of success. The lucky numbers kept coming up, and he kept disregarding them, with the end result that today, in his middle years, he is deeply unhappy in his profession.

There are many teachers who are amongst the most successful and satisfied people in this country. The important thing to consider is that our man neither was successful in his work nor was he content. And when opportunities for a change came his way, he was so negative in his outlook that he shrugged them off. His failure stemmed entirely from his *not knowing what to do* with the chances offered him.

Success: Three Definitions

Before going any further in the discussion of success, some definitions are mandatory.

I see the term success divided into three categories:

1. *Personal Success*
2. *Public Success*
3. *Personal-Public Success*

Let's take the first example.

There is a man who stands in the lobby of the Hotel George V in Paris and he does nothing all day long but give the revolving door a gentle shove. He also greets people.

This man is an extraordinary *Personal Success*. He is loved and, in some ways, worshipped by his family and friends, whom he in turn adores. Upon entering the lobby of the George V, those who know him greet him warmly. They are cheered by his amiable, pleasant face. He is not subservient; nor is he aloof; he is merely the kind of unusual person who makes people happier the moment they see him. He has enormous affection for his work, and it shows through everything he does.

I once drummed up enough courage to ask this doorman whether he envied the countless number of millionaires who rush in and out of the lobby of the hotel. He merely looked at me, a little puzzled. Then he smiled and shrugged, remarking in French, "What would be the point?"

There really was no point. He was a thoroughly satisfied individual—a *Personal Success*.

Personal Success, therefore, should be defined as follows:

The achievement of an inner satisfaction in one's own life not dependent *upon recognition by society*.

Now let's move to the second definition:

The term *Public Success* should be defined as follows:

The attainment of wealth, favour, or eminence as generally recognized by society.

Several years ago, the president of a famous corporation astonished the world by taking his own life. He died, leaving an estate valued at more than $8,000,000 (£2,850,000).

Until his death, there were many who admired his wealth, fame, and corporate power. Whatever drove him to suicide was never made public. He had, perhaps, some deeply rooted sense of his own inadequacy or an overwhelming lack of inner contentment. Obviously, he was a *Public Success*, but not a *Personal Success*.

And finally we come to the term *Personal-Public Success*, a combination of both:

The achievement of an inner contentment coupled with recognition by society.

Only a small percentage of people ever attains this highest degree of fulfilment, but with the proper approach it *can* be attained. Individuals in every profession, in every career, with every conceivable success goal have proved this to be true.

I do not intend to give a copy of this book to the doorman of the Hotel George V. As far as I know, he has no need of it. This book is written for the person who wants to attain *Personal-Public Success*, the man who is not completely satisfied with the life he leads and hopes to change it. He may want to become head of the New York Board of Education.

He may want to be recognized as a major financier, or to rise to the chairmanship of a big company. The field itself is secondary, for the formula for success is virtually the same in all fields. The important thing is that he wants to be an outstanding member of his chosen field. Not only does he want to attain the highest inner satisfaction, he is also determined to attain the full meaning of the *Personal-Public Success:* recognition by society.

Now that we have established our concept of the term Personal-Public Success, we are ready to examine the process of achieving that success.

The first step in this process is this: we must explore ourselves rather well. We must acquaint ourselves with the personality traits we possess, traits which may help or hinder us and possibly make their appearance in our lives when we least expect them.

But exactly what are these traits we tend to label *assets* and *liabilities* of our personalities? And how important are they in the pursuit of our goals?

A favourite premise of psychologists and philosophers is that we can never really know ourselves completely. But I believe we can at least discover enough that is important about ourselves to make that journey towards success ultimately rewarding. I believe we can analyse ourselves, in this regard, by using what is essentially a simple method.

Now let us explore in detail what that method is.

2 Self-Analysis: The Key to Finding Your Goal

WHEN SOME PEOPLE GO TO A CINEMA, THEY WEEP WHEN THE lovers are reunited. I can remember myself weeping once or twice when a character in a film achieved a remarkable success.

Now this may sound like so much nonsense. But in my case, as in the case of many successful people I've met in my life, success actually becomes a beautiful and, in some ways, deeply moving thing. Often, the creation of a particular success may appear like a creation of a magnificent work of art—beautifully wrought, skilfully carried out to its ultimate fruition and achieving striking originality.

Common sense tells us that before we can achieve anything in life, we must know whether or not we really want that "anything".

For years, psychologists have expounded at great length on the type of person who has a particular desire, achieves the fulfilment of that desire and then, once he has what he wants, no longer wants it. But what of the even sadder individual who deludes himself into thinking he wants something and *never* achieves it? This poor soul is forced into an even more frustrating position, for he never finds out for himself how little the object meant to him in the first place.

So many people *claim* they want to be successful because they imagine it's the way to be. They will struggle and grope in one area after the other, trying to achieve what holds very little real interest for them and continuing to live in the particular fantasy world of their choice. Sometimes, they complain about the way the gods have cheated them. They go about foolishly envying the ones who have "made it," downgrading the talent of these other individuals and putting all their real energy into self-pity.

I once heard a rather ironic story about a man of this type who, by the age of forty, had actually convinced all his friends that the only reason he couldn't begin his own wholesale clothing business was that he didn't have sufficient funds to make the necessary investment. He had marvellous dreams about what he could do if he were only given the chance. His promotional schemes sounded excellent, and he had descended so deeply into his particular fantasy that he had even drawn up on paper an interminable list of contacts for the proposed enterprise, including the names of clothing manufacturers, top advertising agencies that specialized in men's fashion, and sales executives from other firms who would be willing to go to work for him.

Unfortunately, however, this man had been forced into a job which provided him with too little salary for him to save enough money to make the required investment. At least *that* was what he told the others!

Well, one afternoon he was relating the usual account of his hapless life (by this time, I'm sure, it had reached the point where it contained an assortment of embellishments to make the story even more convincing) when quite unexpectedly the man to whom he was telling his tale of woe looked him straight in the eye and said, quite simply, "All right, I think I can be the one to provide you with the necessary capital."

The first reaction of the would-be clothier was disbelief. But when the other man pointed out in detail how he had been considering an investment of this kind for several months, the man seemed overjoyed. He couldn't believe his change of luck! At last the gods had decided to make up for all the wrong they had done him in previous years.

Several weeks passed after the meeting between the two men, but the man who had offered to put up the necessary capital had failed to hear from his friend. Indeed, it seemed puzzling! For here at last a financier was offering to turn a lifelong dream into a reality. Yet, the financier had not received as much as a telephone call from the other individual.

Finally, the financier decided to investigate matters for himself. When he couldn't reach the other man on the telephone, he began to grow worried and called mutual friends in the hope that they would provide the necessary explanation.

They did. The reason for the would-be clothier's disappearance turned out to be shocking.

The first thing he had done after the financier had made his promise was to leave his job, convinced that now he would be embarking on a new and exciting career. But then, within a matter of days, odd things began to happen. The would-be clothier had apparently become filled with inexplicable fright. He simply could not bring himself to telephone the financier, and began drinking so heavily that before very long he became almost entirely uncommunicative. The drinking grew steadily worse, and now he was staying at the home of some members of his family who were convinced he was headed for a complete nervous breakdown.

As sad as this story is, it is not unusual. In fact, some of our great literature abounds with the theme of the pipe dream. The typical story or play built around this premise deals with the character who fills his own head and the heads of others with tales about the great things he might accomplish if only given the opportunity. Unfortunately, when the opportunity does arise, it explodes the pipe dream like so much hot air and leads the character to tragedy.

Ask yourself the question, then: *Is success something I really want?*

And don't be too hasty supplying an answer. Give yourself plenty of time to think about it.

Try to recall opportunities for success that have already occurred in your life. How did you react at the time? Did you quickly dismiss these opportunities as hopeless? Did you do something which spoiled your chances of making the opportunities materialize? Or did the opportunities legitimately slip out of your grasp?

In the previous chapter, I discussed my concept of the term *Personal Success* and the type of individual who is aware of the fact that he wants nothing more than to lead a very average or below-average existence, with just enough money for himself and his family to live on and a comfortable if unexciting job. This sort of person at least recognizes what is true about himself: he doesn't want real success, he has no need for it. And he is right: *why should he have something he does not want?*

But what about yourself? You must realize that in order to achieve your dreamed-of success, that dream has to be part of a basic desire within you, not just a vague groping. You must feel that your life *cannot be complete without it.*

You must love the idea of success.

By this I mean that when you hear of the success of another man, you must feel *admiration* and a kind of *empathy*. If it's jealousy you feel—well, let that be your first clue to tell you that you are probably not the kind of individual really interested in becoming a success.

As far back as I can remember in my own life, I never had any doubt that I wanted success of some sort or another. When I learned of the successes of other people, I never recall finding myself filled with envy. My initial reaction took the form of admiration. Then that reaction turned to curiosity. How did the individual become so successful? I would ask myself. What were the steps he took which led him to his present status in life?

Do you have the same reaction when you hear of another man's success? Or are you inclined to say he is merely lucky, blaming your own failure on an absence of luck?

Once you have made up your mind to answer realistically, you can proceed to other steps. But without this initial determination on your part to face the facts about yourself and to see whether you are the kind of individual who truly wants success, you soon will become lost.

Here then is our first rule:

Examine your desire for success realistically.

One evening several years ago, the son of a distant relative came to see me about a problem he was having in trying to decide on a career for himself. The young man had just received an M.A. in Business Administration, but his years of college had miraculously failed to provide him with a single clue as to what profession he might enter.

All he knew was he wanted to go into some area of what he loosely termed "business". I mentioned the stock market to him. He smiled and said he had thought about it. Then I told him about a job opening I knew of which happened to be on the executive staff of a large dress manufacturing company. He smiled again and said it did not sound like a bad idea. I also threw a suggestion about banking at him. And then I hinted that he might enjoy a position in the canning industry.

He greeted all suggestions fairly warmly and seemed willing to go along with any idea I had to offer him, though he failed to express that extra spark of interest which would make any of these possibilities appear really worth exploring.

Suddenly, I realized I had taken the wrong approach with this young man. Instead of asking him what he *might* enjoy doing, I decided to ask him what he *already* enjoyed doing— *and did well.*

At first, the young man reacted to my question in a puzzled manner. Then, almost as if he considered it a joke, he began to tell me how much he loved sports. While studying for his degree, he said, he had been a star basketball player at his college.

I asked him what else he enjoyed doing, and he mentioned several other hobbies. But he kept drifting back to sports as being his primary source of interest and amusement.

I began to consider the possibilities as they drifted into my mind. Would he make a good professional athlete?

It didn't seem likely, for he had his M.A. in Business Administration and hadn't played his major sport—basketball—for more than a year.

Suppose, then, he tried to land a job as a sportswriter? But the young man showed little interest in writing of any kind, much less journalism.

Taking into full account the nature of his degree and the source of study to which he had devoted a number of years—coupled with his extraordinary interest in sports of all varieties—I finally arrived at the right answer. I asked him if he had looked into the possibility of securing a job as an executive with a firm that manufactured sporting goods. He was certainly one step ahead of the applicant fresh from college who had little interest in athletic activities.

Strangely enough, the young man had not even given any thought to the fact that such firms existed. To this young man the term "business executive" seemed to imply dealings with brokerage houses or real-estate firms. I pointed out that the manufacture of sporting goods was among the most lucrative businesses in the United States and mentioned a few company names to him.

After leaving me, the young man wrote less than a dozen letters to the personnel departments of these companies. In his letters, he mentioned his lack of job experience but pointed out his great love of sports and how he felt that, because of it, there was already a basis of interest in working for this type of firm.

Obviously, at least one of his letters had created the desired effect, for within weeks the young man landed a job with a top outfit.

In considering what you are cut out for, in what profession you are likely to succeed, it's a lot easier choosing an area which has absorbed at least some of your interest. Sometimes, it doesn't even matter that the interest is small. As long as it's there, you know you are headed in a plausible direction.

34

I approve wholeheartedly of aptitude tests. But a more simple formula would be:

Let your goal grow out of what you like to do.

You may not even have to bother trying out new things.

Consider your hobbies. They are usually the best things you can start with, for there is nothing more representative of what people like to do than the things they do *without getting paid for doing them.*

A young man, let's say, is an avid reader of mystery fiction. Copies of the latest suspense thriller are barely on the shelves of his local bookstore a week before the young man has purchased one for himself. The young man knows, too, that he has a certain amount of talent in writing. He's read a sufficient number of mystery novels to realize the correct formulas for himself. Then why not develop his writing talent further by taking a few courses in fiction writing? But the idea would be for him not to try experimenting in five different writing forms. The idea would be for him to concentrate entirely on turning out a completed mystery novel. It is in that direction —and that direction alone—that his real success seems to lie.

Another man has a dismal job in an office. Why is it dismal? It certainly pays well enough, and this man has displayed sufficient talent to be considered adept at handling matters pertaining to the office. It's simply dismal because he doesn't like the kind of products with which he is forced to involve himself. Meanwhile, he has spent nearly every hour at week-ends toying around with mechanical parts in his garage. It would make sense, then, for him to leave his present position and look for one in a field related directly with mechanics. In this particular area, he can combine his solid business know-how with the hobby he loves most. And the chances are that, since *he will like what he is doing*, he will become truly successful.

Of course, these cases may appear oversimplified. But they illustrate the principle. These two men are taking what they enjoy doing and applying it to their particular goals.

There is the case of a world-famous beauty expert who has astounded countless women with her uncomplicated but quite remarkable beauty and high-fashion hints in her daily newspaper column. The woman began her career as a very average reporter on her newspaper, making a very average newspaperwoman's salary. One day, however, she came to a somewhat startling realization about herself. She knew she was not what would be considered a conventionally beautiful woman; yet people were constantly commenting on how attractive she looked. When she compared herself to other women in the newspaper office, she recognized objectively that many of them had features far more delicate and figures much better shaped than her own. But the compliments directed at her far outnumbered those received by the women she considered lovelier than herself.

The realization this woman came to was that she had a knack—a knack which few women writers she knew seemed to have. It was a knack for underplaying her less attractive physical qualities and emphasizing her more attractive ones. Suddenly, the idea occurred to her: why not turn this thing she did so well, this little hobby of appearing beautiful, into something more significant as far as her ultimate goal was concerned?

She wanted, as most newspaper people do, her own by-line, her own prestige. In order to attain both these luxuries she had to do something which would distinguish her from others in her field. And so, one morning, she knocked on her publisher's door and announced her idea for a beauty column that would be somewhat different from other columns which had appeared in that newspaper: it would merely tell the readers, as simply and as straightforwardly as possible, *how to be beautiful without really trying.*

The publisher loved her ideas for the column, and in no time at all the woman scored an enormous success. This writer had learned through her own experience that one of the best ways to become successful is to apply what you like to do and what you do well to your own career. Let us repeat then our second rule:

Let your goal grow out of what you like to do.

Ask yourself the simple question: *What else do I need besides success?*

Now this may sound elementary on the surface, but consider the facts of your life. You know quite well that the goal you choose will not be sufficient to make you a completely satisfied, well-rounded individual.

I once knew a man who, like so many individuals, had made his primary goal in life *money.* But he hadn't taken the trouble to think out wisely and methodically exactly under what circumstances that money was to be made. He had a good salary, working at a reasonably pleasant, full-time job during the day, but at night and week-ends he carried out an exhausting, emotionally enervating business from his own home. Naturally, he liked the cash this second business brought, but he had little time to enjoy his life with his family and the pleasures which free time could bring. All this overwork had a depressing effect on him and, ironically, he lost interest in his full-time position and eventually was replaced in the job by somebody else.

There are some people who are never able to relax. They are happiest possibly when they are involved in a hectic, even exhausting, project at the office. To them there simply is no conflict between their success drives and their moments of diversion. But to the man I've described, diversion was as necessary as the *very rudiments* of his success drive. Yet, he had made the mistake of not analysing his needs fully. He failed to take into consideration one of the most important factors upon which his *particular* success depended: his family life.

In studying his case carefully, one comes to the conclusion that he was so wrapped up in the *idea* of making money, he had not even bothered to consider his means of doing so. He had foolishly turned himself into a desperate man, snatching at any financial opportunity which came his way, regardless of the emotional burdens it might thrust upon him.

Let's consider another case—a hypothetical one.

A man realizes, without having to delve into any lengthy analysis of his needs, that travel represents something more to him than a pleasant pastime. In its own way, it revitalizes him, renews his strength to carry out a successful career. He, therefore, knows that he must use at least eight weeks out of the year for seeing an area of the world where he has never previously been.

Someone looking at his case superficially may say, "But why doesn't he devote all those extra weeks to building his career?"

The point is he *couldn't* build his career effectively unless travel was a sufficient part of his over-all existence. This man wisely knows that, once returned from a particular trip, his head is filled with brighter, newer, and more creative ideas about how to run his business. And in the long run, this man realizes, he will become a greater success by fulfilling all the needs his individual personality requires.

This explains why, for example, the President of the United

States is actually *under orders* to relax for certain periods of time. The underlying reason behind this is fairly obvious: once relieved of fatigue and overwork, the President is better able to carry out his duties.

So, here is an important rule in analysing yourself in terms of your goal:

Don't overlook personal needs.

You may discover that some of your personal needs come into drastic conflict with your primary goal (as they did with the individual whose life was devoted to the pursuit of money). By looking into *all* of your needs, however, you will be getting closer to what you really want. And before very long, you will discover the best possible way to bring these needs into harmony with your primary goal.

How to Be Successful Even Though You Stutter

Without meaning to insult the reader's intelligence, I think I should point out that the above heading sounds like a joke but isn't. Examine it a moment. Is it as absurd as it may appear?

Many of us have found ourselves within a promising situation, yet somehow we do not make the best of that situation simply because a negative trait we happen to possess seems to stand in the way.

When I was considering entering show business for the very first time, I kept reminding myself that, though I loved the idea of entertaining an audience, I might find myself incapable of doing so. The reason I believed this to be true was based on a deeply rooted conviction: I was painfully and irrevocably shy.

Therefore, I had a choice of doing one of two things: I

39

could immediately dismiss the idea of entertaining an audience as a frustrating pipe dream—or I could find some way to get up there under the lights and perform *while remaining shy.*

The thought of ridding myself of my shyness never entered into my thinking. But many people who do not possess the characteristics they feel a particular profession requires will go out of their way to try to possess them. Have you ever encountered, for example, the awkward, stumbling matron who takes it upon herself to be a hostess at a charity function? Chances are she makes you feel twice as uncomfortable as you might have felt had she not greeted you at all. In a sense, perhaps, this woman is a victim of too much positive thinking. She is probably so determined to be the "proper hostess" that she keeps saying over and over in her own mind, "I must be gracious. I must be extroverted. I must keep smiling and laughing." By the time the charity function begins, her anxiety has probably assumed such gigantic proportions she loses whatever quiet charm she might, in reality, possess.

In my particular case, I knew there was little chance of getting rid of my shyness. I decided I simply had to live with it. Consequently, I developed a type of act where I did not have to come into contact with the public on a real emotional level. And so I became a dancer. There I was, very active in the pursuance of my goal: I was under the lights and before an audience—*in spite of my shyness.*

Let's take another seemingly "negative" character trait.

Do you consider yourself a *coward?* If so, in what way are you cowardly? If you happen to be an executive of General Motors, no one will ask you to crawl beneath barbed wire with bullets flying over your head. On the other hand, perhaps you are afraid of taking on business responsibilities.

Self-Analysis: The Key to Finding Your Goal

If that is the case, then may I suggest you not consider going to work for General Motors?

It's as simple as this:

Be strong enough to recognise your weaknesses.

Molière was one of the greatest authors of comedy who ever lived. Yet he insisted on writing an occassional tragedy, which turned out to be an abysmal failure. Had he merely recognized the fact that his writing tragedy was based on an unreal estimate of his own talent, he might have saved himself the time and anguish which these unsuccessful plays brought him.

Einstein was one of our great geniuses. But he did not know how to fill out an Internal Revenue form. He recognized his inadequacy in this particular area and left *that* job to others more experienced than he.

As cheerfully as you admit to yourself the things you do know, you must admit to yourself the things you do *not* know. In some ways, by doing this, you may achieve even greater self-assurance. And occasionally, you will find your faults will turn to virtues.

A man may not be a great lover, but he immediately has a certain extra charm to a woman if he is aware of this fact. His chances of succeeding with his beloved are far greater if he makes no attempt to become a combination of Charles Boyer and Richard Burton.

I know so many would-be actors and actresses who imagine they have sufficient talent to become successful either on Broadway or in films. But perhaps these dozens of frustrated actors and actresses could be leading far more rewarding lives by choosing other areas of theatre as their job goals.

I have a friend who inherited a considerable amount of money, but in investing it, he consistently makes wrong judgments in whatever area of business he happens to choose. Now this is the irony of his predicament: he is constantly choosing business roles which require the most delicately balanced, dangerously precise decision-making. I do not think I have to point out how long his inherited fortune will last.

Thus, we come to another important rule:

Make sure your particular talent for success is directed towards its most promising goal.

Let's take the case of Freddie Bartholomew, an enormously popular (to use our phrase) *Personal-Public Success* as a child star. Bartholomew, for whatever reason—and it may have nothing whatsoever to do with the measure of his acting talent—has selected an entirely new field for himself in recent years: advertising. He is now, once again, a *Personal-Public Success*, though in an entirely different area.

Perhaps Bartholomew was wise enough to realize the problems facing today's actor who wants to stay on top. Perhaps he explored his other aptitudes and discovered the one which is now fulfilling him as a successful adult.

George Murphy might have had a difficult time of it building a career as a star in today's film world, but he is now a United States Senator.

In considering one's most promising goal, there is a subsidary rule which might be termed as follows:

Don't set your goal beyond your capacity.

I was once very surprised to learn that the husband of a close friend of mine from Hungary was no longer working for a large whisky distilling company, a firm where he had been employed for more than fifteen years. My friend's husband had been enormously successful as a sales manager. As far as I knew, he had never had any intention of leaving the whisky firm, and it struck me as unlikely that the company would sack a man who had been so effective in his particular sales capacity.

When I asked my friend what had happened to make her husband leave the position, she told me the following sad story:

Her husband had been one of the top sales managers in his field; he had loved his job and made a superb salary. For years, however, he had built up the dream of one day becoming vice-president of his firm. His sights were set on a goal which obviously had very little basis in reality, for the moment his company decided to promote him to the higher position—the moment he had to handle responsibilities he had never dreamed a vice-president had—he became wary and afraid. Within a year after his appointment as vice-president, he lost the job.

What's really tragic about this particular case is that had this man analysed in his own mind the kind of hurdles he would have to surmount once he became vice-president, he probably never would have tried to achieve that position in the first place. Unfortunately, his striving to reach a goal beyond his actual capacity finished his career, and the man is now in a subsidiary selling job with another company.

An important thing to keep in mind when you decide on a particular goal is to determine exactly how qualified you are to meet its requirements. And make sure that it's not too high to reach. Remember that a man without a job is worse off than one who has a job in a lesser capacity than the one which the dream-world image of himself appears to tell him he can fill.

Now let's turn to our final and perhaps most important rule: *Direct your mind to what is relevant.*

A friend of mine, an inventor, once develped a revolutionary new washing powder which he demonstrated before a large group of manufacturers' representatives. A short while after the demonstration, my friend telephoned me frantically and, cursing his luck, announced how badly the demonstration had gone.

I was puzzled as to what had gone wrong, for my friend had demonstrated the washing powder for me himself and it seemed to work most effectively.

"Oh, that part of it went all right," said my friend in an offhand manner. "It's just that I become so painfully shy in front of a group like that."

His statement amused me considerably, but I decided to hold back my laughter for fear it would upset him. Instead, I asked if he thought he had convinced the manufacturers' representatives that the product worked. "I suppose so," my friend sadly replied, as if that part of it hardly mattered.

"Well, don't you think the only important thing was whether or not the washing powder took the dirt out?" I said. "If you were simply a salesman, that would be one thing. But after all, the salesman's job is not to invent. The only thing you were really responsible for today was pouring the soap powder and water over the soiled clothes."

At that point, my friend laughed at the absurdity of his own reaction. But all he had done, actually, was react the way a great many of us react when we are concerned over irrelevant aspects of our personalities.

How many of us, in fact, spend countless hours during the course of a week worrying over inconsequential things?

I once knew a very successful woman insurance representative who had just landed a much-sought-after account, but spent an entire week-end moping over the fact that she had made dinner for a group of former business acquaintances and had burned the entire meal. Had she treated the matter lightly, her old friends would have done the same. She could quite easily have laughed off the homemade dinner as a fiasco and have taken her guests to dine in a fine restaurant, for the new account had provided her with a sufficient advance to buy several hundred dinners in fine restaurants. Instead of doing what should have appeared obvious, she fretted and fumed, scolding herself for her own carelessness, treating the irrelevant matter as a relevant one.

Let's suppose you would like to become a successful opera singer. In that case, all that's important really is to know whether you have a "voice." And that's a fact not terribly difficult to discover. If you do not have a voice and still want to be an opera singer, perhaps an authority in this field can advise you as to whether that voice can be developed. Suppose, however, the answer is still on the negative side. No voice—and no chance of obtaining one! The solution should appear obvious: choose another field.

But if you happen to be a rather short person and are concerned whether this factor should deter you from entering the operatic field, the point is, needless to say, irrelevant.

Let's examine the hypothetical case of a particular individual and the goal he hopes to reach. Let's call him Frank Rivers.

Mr. Rivers wants—let us say, for exaggeration's sake—to become chairman of a steel company. Mr Rivers begins to examine his liabilities. The first thing that comes to mind is that he has a noticeable limp as the result of a car accident. It is obviously the liability which bothers him more than any other, so he lists that particular one first:

Have a physical disability.

He thinks about things he has done poorly and lists the liabilities they reveal:

Am a poor host.

Am lacking in artistic sense.

He remembers the time he was asked to address the local branch of a club on the importance of raising money for a particular charity. He recalls how he fumbled nervously during the speech, persuading no one of anything.

Therefore, he lists:

Am below-average speaker.

He also considers the low marks he received in English composition classes while he was attending college. He lists:

Am a bad writer.

Now he turns to his assets. The picture changes brightly. At the club, he may have made a bad speech, lacking in persuasive power, but he certainly managed to raise money for the campaign by talking to friends and associates *privately*. People seemed to listen to what he had to say. On several occasions, he planned theatrical and dinner outings for more than a hundred club members. The outings proved to be most successful. People were moved by his ideas. And the ideas seemed to work. He was also very adept in taking over his office on the numerous occasions when his boss was out of town.

Therefore, he lists under *Assets:*

Have the ability to lead others.

Have the ability to handle responsibility.

He recalls other business experiences he has carried out successfully and he continues his list as follows:

Have an encompassing view of things—am able to foresee how business situations will develop.

Have a good technical sense.

Am capable of making decisions and sticking by them.

Let us consider, then, his brief list. In looking over the liabilities, we can dismiss at once the one which, ironically, seems to bother Mr. Rivers the most—the physical one.

Am a poor host. Well, there may be some occasions when

this could prove slightly disadvantageous, but it is not very important.

Am lacking in artistic sense. Not too important.

Am below-average speaker. This may have *some* importance. But when we start to consider the number of fine men in important positions who also happened to have been weak speechmakers, we are able to dismiss this liability rather quickly.

Am a bad writer. Some importance but not too much. There is bound to be a sizable portion of staff well-equipped to take care of the actual writing of business reports.

We turn now to his list of assets. They are all extremely favourable, extremely promising. They far outweigh the liabilities in Mr. Rivers' pursuit of his particular goal.

Of course it is impossible to say whether Mr. Rivers will ever achieve his goal and become chairman of a steel company. But at least one significant factor is clear: he has analysed himself to know that he has some of the important assets which obviously such an individual must possess.

Here, then, is the list of rules for us to follow while analysing ourselves in terms of our success goals:

1. *Examine your desire for success realistically.*

2. *Let your goal grow out of what you like to do.*

3. *Don't overlook personal needs.*

4. *Be strong enough to recognize your weaknesses.*

5. *Make sure your particular talent for success is directed towards its most promising goal.*

6. *Don't set your goal beyond your capacity.*

7. *Direct your mind to what is relevant.*

Now that we have what I hope is at least a moderately sound concept of ourselves, in terms of what kind of success we want, we are ready to approach a different kind of analysis: an analysis of the field in which we will find ourselves and, even more important, an analysis of the best possible method of achieving success in that field.

At first examination, a situation may seem pretty hopeless. But hopelessness begins to diminish and possibly even vanish once we recognize what our particular problems are and explore in detail how we can cope with them.

Quite often, during my own life, I have been involved in this type of analysis. At various stages, I wanted to be successful in areas where I had not, as yet, received an ounce of recognition, much less encouragement.

I faced this kind of predicament in June, 1943, in what was probably the most dramatic point in my life. War had just broken out in my homeland, Hungary, and I left that country and travelled to Turkey. When I arrived at Istanbul, I had no job, little cash, no knowledge of the Turkish language, and no Turkish citizenship. In addition, I had no close acquaintances in that country who might have helped me—and I had no profession upon which to rely for a future income.

In short, my situation appeared—at least on the surface—to be entirely bad. I had the feeling that if I were to jump in the Bosporus, no one would take the trouble to fish me out. My existence seemed utterly without significance.

Nevertheless, I had learned early in life that when one has a strong drive in the direction of success, one's problems can be solved.

I should like to review, in brief, my approach to my predicament in the year 1943 for an important reason: to give you an example of the approach you yourself will have to make to whatever success goal you would like to obtain.

48

Self-Analysis: The Key to Finding Your Goal

Here is how I not only solved the seemingly insurmountable problems of my situation at that particular time but went on to turn my dreams into a reality that would not have seemed, at least in the beginning, anything more than the wildest product of an active imagination.

3 Success: *Its Best Possible Route*

NOW THERE I WAS IN TURKEY IN 1943. I KNEW I HAD TO move quickly in order to avoid starvation, which was, of course, an even more pressing problem than directing myself towards a particular success goal.

The first step I took, in analysing my situation, was to think about doing those things I did well and enjoyed doing. I considered a number of my attributes. A few professions and job ideas entered into my mind, but I dismissed them rather quickly.

Then I began to think about one of my strongest desires —to do something significant in the entertainment field. As I have mentioned before, I had to bear in mind my shyness, and so I decided that a dancing act would be best for my particular type of personality.

But merely to be a *successful* professional dancer? Was

that *all* I wanted? No, I wanted something even greater. Why not set up an even more stunning goal for myself? Why not become a *world-famous* professional dancer?

Gradually, the idea took shape. I began to consider, roughly, what I might have to do to achieve such a goal. In analysing the path I would take, I realized that while the goal itself was single, the path would be twofold:

1. To *develop* sufficient talent to become a good dancer; and

2. To build a career through *selling* this talent properly.

I knew I could never achieve my ultimate goal unless I travelled both these paths. Had I, for example, concentrated merely on developing my talent, I would have stayed in Turkey, with a number of engagements at Turkey's top night spots, but I would have also remained obscure to the rest of the world.

The moment I embarked on the first pathway—to develop my talent—I began rehearsing every day, practising the latest dance steps and studying in great detail the current conditions of the dancing field. I also began buying international publications devoted to the dancing profession and learned about the styles of world-famous dancers and the cities where these dancers appeared. Two of these cities seemed to stand out as significant rungs on the dancer's career ladder: Paris and New York. Soon it became apparent that the city which was most likely to present me with my goal was New York. Paris was merely an important stepping-stone.

I realized that in order to be accepted eventually by a New York audience I would have to find out what New Yorkers—and possibly most Americans—enjoyed. I, therefore, began spending at least three full afternoons a week going to American films. I tried to learn from these not only the type of dancing which was most popular in the United States but also the trends in audience response.

I noticed little patterns which began to repeat themselves. At first, these patterns had no meaning for me. But soon I began to see them in relationship to dancing itself. For example, in gangster films, I observed that when someone fired a gun, he hardly ever fired one bullet—there was always a *succession* of bullets. The effect was apparently considered more dramatic. I thought of this in terms of my choreography.

I also noticed that American films, regardless of their particular genre, were filled with suspense and surprise. The leisurely paced, seemingly uneventful motion picture was obviously not in fashion. I, therefore, came to the conclusion that Americans wanted suspense and surprise, and I created my choreography accordingly.

But my dancing act was merely my merchandise. Now I had to sell it!

And so I turned to the second pathway: making myself known.

The direction I hoped to follow in this instance appeared like a serpentine route, marked off by various stop signs.

The first stop sign appeared where I was now: *Turkey.*

The route continued, passing through other cities of the Middle East and Europe. The second stop sign read: *Paris.* And the third and final sign, where my goal was to be attained, read: *New York.*

The route itself was long, but not nearly as long as one might think. I knew that it would be impossible for me to visit every city in Europe; it was merely necessary to secure jobs in three or four important cities within an individual country.

Of course, I also had to consider a fundamental problem.

I knew the tremendous value of publicity and advertising

in helping me land these jobs, but I had no financial resources with which to cover this promotional area. What was I to do? I did the next best thing. I invented a kind of mail-order show business.

This is how I worked it: I gathered together the names and addresses of the most important and influential theatrical agents, night-club owners, and theatre managers around the world and wrote countless numbers of letters to them. I described what I was doing, sent photographs of my act and let them know where I was performing. Also, I enclosed my own publicity releases of my engagements. In fact, I made absolutely certain that they received *something* with my name on it at least once a week. They *had* to take notice of me!

Thus, I had analysed my situation. I had surveyed the terrain, and started to proceed on the best possible route to success.

Now, Turkish citizenship notwithstanding, my future did not appear half so dismal.

Now That You Know Yourself, Do You Know What You're In For?

I do not imagine, at the present time, you are stuck in Turkey with little money and no profession. But let's assume you are stuck somewhere—in a situation not entirely to your liking. You've already analysed *yourself*; you have examined the character assets and liabilities you possess; and you see, at least roughly, how they apply to your particular goal.

Now you are ready to go to the next important step: to analyse the *situation*.

Let us imagine you are a sales representative for a large corporation and your goal is to become a top executive in the business world. Through self-analysis, you have discovered that you possess a number of personality traits necessary to this particular goal. Among other things, you have learned that you have an ability to generate new and creative ideas within your organization. You have also discovered that you have a greater capacity for carrying out your own ideas to their successful conclusion than for following ideas generated by other individuals. Yet, you are stifled because you have several supervisors over you, all telling you what to do—and sometimes the advice is contradictory.

You feel that you must escape from this untenable situation. You are certain, once you assume more responsibility on a job, you will be more successful.

After analysing the particular area in which you have had sales experience, you may come to the realization that you would have similar problems working for any firm of comparable size. Of course, the temptation to work at a large firm is great, simply because of the prestige involved. But do you love prestige that much when the cost is so high?

Suddenly, a new consideration enters into the picture. Why not look for a job *within the same sales area but with a smaller firm?*

Perhaps the salary may be a bit lower than what you are making now, but in a small firm, where you will assume more responsibility (and you will want to make sure that you *will* before you accept the job), you can start carrying out your own creative ideas without having to depend on five or six people to guide you. You consider the fact that there are a number of wonderful things you can do once you are hired by this small organization. If your ideas are good enough, you will find the firm growing by leaps and bounds with you as one of its guides. Before you know it, the firm may even be on the same level as a larger firm—only now, *you* will be giving the orders.

Then, you consider still another possibility. Suppose this smaller firm, for whatever the cause may be, simply does not expand? Well, after a year or two of acting in a supervisory capacity at a small firm, you could safely request a job in a similar capacity at a larger firm. Over the longer period of time, you are still making greater progress than you might have made by remaining at the large organization.

What is so significant about what you have done is that, in analysing yourself, you have found what you are best cut out for: working for a smaller firm because you like to carry out *your own ideas*! *Taking* orders is not your strongest point, while *giving* them is.

Thus, we have come to our first important rule in analysing the direction we plan to follow:

Go over in your own mind your assets and liabilities, as you have learned them through self-analysis, and see how they apply to your particular goal.

After you have done this, you may decide that you are in the wrong job spot—and a change is forthcoming.

In reviewing the steps I took before embarking full-scale on a career as a dancer, I analysed the field itself rather thoroughly. I tried to learn something about the kind of individuals who worked in that field. Later, too, when my dancing act became more acrobatic, I discovered the odd fact that other acrobatic dancers seemed to be limited in their ability to intellectualize a situation. I knew that I would have the advantage over them because I intellectualized nearly everything. If it came to it, I could outwit a competing acrobatic dancer merely by using my brain and knowing when and where to make the next move in furthering my career.

Let us take, for a moment, a kind of success which has

nothing whatever to do with a job or a career—a goal which some people have pursued with such energy and drive one would imagine their weary lives depended on its achievement: the goal of success through *social climbing*.

Though the purpose of this goal may be entirely incongruous with the type of success we are discussing in this book, the steps one has to take to achieve it are relatively the same as those in any career field.

The first thing you would have to discover for yourself is exactly what the social set is, and to do this you would have to start reading the society columns in the daily newspapers. After a while, you would see that the same names keep appearing and reappearing, names which are somehow linked with one another. The columns you read would soon stick in your memory and you would know which names of the so-called "smart set" belong with which other names. You would know who is engaged to whom and who has just taken a third wife, together with the name of the latter's former husband.

Above all, you would find yourself dining where these celebrities are dining. Sometimes, you would even read about someone whom you yourself know and who, in turn, could introduce you to the people who will ultimately aid your success goal.

Surely, if you or your escort could afford it, you would start to go to the top restaurants and night clubs. You would also learn who should accompany you to these places.

Once you have started making appearances at these exclusive places, your chances of becoming a social success would be 75 per cent better than would the person's who is accidentally taken to one of these places for the celebration of a birthday or anniversary.

Suppose, then, that you are a young lady who wants to meet and marry a millionaire (and I know several young women who have found husbands exactly in this manner). You will find out on which night your prospective husband will be at which night spot. You will learn where he likes to sit, and you will try to secure a table not far from his. Your research may also have resulted in a number of important physical considerations. You have discovered, for example, that he prefers blondes, and you will become one for the evening. In fact, once you make his acquaintance, you may even decide to *remain* a blonde!

All of the preceding may strike the reader as a somewhat cold-blooded approach directed towards a less than admirable goal. But an important thing to consider is that the approach surprisingly often works. A similar approach, when applied to becoming president of a corporation—or, for that matter, the United States—may strike you as less cold-blooded simply because the goal is more praiseworthy.

All right, then, let us assume you want to be the country's primary leader. You would, once again, explore the field and recognize your potential rivals. You would study the careers of other Presidents. You would learn how candidates achieved their political power and dominated the country's limelight. Perhaps a candidate was the senator from a heavily populated state. See how he sponsored a number of important bills in Congress. Watch how he developed his image. Recognize how his ideals and party programmes coincided with the ideals and programmes of the majority of voters. Analyse how he got into the headlines.

No matter how idealistic a presidential candidate may be, he is bound to recognize how his own particular theories and precepts will win him votes; he also knows which of these ideas he may have to eliminate, or at least temporarily disregard, before he can win the favour of the voting public at large. With this information clearly analysed in his own mind, he is far ahead of the candidate who is still vague about what the public wants. It is fine to be an idealist—nearly every presidential candidate appears to be—but the candidate must also formulate his ideals into down-to-earth terms which will appeal to his voters.

How are the successful millionaire-hunting young woman and the successful candidate for President similar? They have both thoroughly analysed the area in which they are operating so that they know exactly where and when to make the appropriate moves.

Turning now to fashion, let us suppose you want to be a success in that field. Once again, you will have to survey the territory.

You may decide that you want to work for a top fashion firm. In that case, you must learn which companies are considered the best, what their styles are like, their price ranges, their volume distribution within price ranges, and in what area the popular demand seems to lie. Once you know these things, you will be able to orient your own talents accordingly.

When I was planning to take over a top fashion house, nearly everyone in the field told me I would need at least $200,000 with which to gamble in order to determine whether the new styles of dresses which the house was offering would prove acceptable. I knew, however, that I could make this little test case with a gamble of much less capital: $50,000—*the cost of a fashion show.*

By financing a fashion show for this firm, I could find out very quickly which of the model dresses were most popular with buyers and what my sales projection would be. If none of these model dresses proved popular, my loss was considerable, but comparatively minor when one considers that I might have lost $200,000!

Here, again, I followed the same concept. By presenting a fashion show, I would be giving myself an opportunity to analyse the conditions within a particular field.

It is imperative that you be thoroughly acquainted with any situation you set up for yourself. It is not enough to say, for example, you want to open a men's-wear store. Have other men's-wear stores operated successfully in that part of the town? Is there a need for the type of clothing you are planning to sell?

You must realize, too, that you are going to have to compete in that field against those who are *already successful*. Merely being as good as they are won't be enough. Somewhere along the line, you must be able to offer more than these other individuals.

If you are accurate in your appraisal of the territory, you will invariably find that your competitors have certain shortcomings which, by using your ingenuity, you can overcome in your own business. To become a champion flower-grower, it is more important for you to recognize which flowers your competitors grow poorly than it is for you to know which flowers are grown comparatively well. Then it is up to you to make yourself the one individual who performs wonders with the apparently difficult seedlings. By just entering the field blindly and growing tulips—when tulips happen to be a penny a dozen—you are already setting yourself up for defeat.

All of these examples boil down to our second all-inclusive rule:

Analyse thoroughly the field in which you are planning to succeed.

After analysing the area which contains your success goal, you must proceed to recognize the steps themselves which you have to take in order to achieve success.

Returning to the gardening field as an example, you may have decided that the major weakness of other top flower-growers is their inability to grow perfect orchids. You then decide you will turn yourself into a champion orchid-grower.

First, of course, you must understand how orchids are grown. You must study the market thoroughly, and then you must find out what other orchid-growers are doing that prevents the blooming of perfect specimens.

In the political field, you must know your opponents, their number, their strengths, and their weaknesses. It will probably be necessary to show your voters how you happen to excel in the areas where your opponents fumble.

When I first decided to enter the field of theatrical production, I had my secretary draw up a list of Broadway hits in recent years. I became aware of who wrote them and who the directors were; I noted what impact a star had on a particular production. Then, and only then, did I decide what type of show I might produce, whom I would ask to write it, who would direct, and who would be the star.

When I invested money in the stock market, I recognized that there were clearly defined trends for me to follow. Any competent stock analyst will tell you that stocks of different industries move together, forming certain patterns. If you decide, for example, to invest in an airline company simply because that company happens to represent a strong group at a particular time, you are way ahead of the investor who walks blindly into the broker's office and asks the broker to suggest some good stock.

As you become more and more acquainted with the stock

market, you will recognize which groups are on an uptrend and which are on a downtrend; you will know which stocks are strong and which are weak; and you will be aware of the most preferred stock in the most preferred group.

A man who enters the restaurant business is faced with analysis of a different sort. He must study the location of his restaurant; he must examine which types of restaurants are most successful in that area; and he should also know whether or not to make his restaurant low-priced, medium-priced or high-priced, Italian, French or Chinese.

Here again, you are faced with recognizing conditions within your chosen field. When J&B Scotch proved extraordinarily popular because of its lighter base, other liquor firms began making similar types of scotch. Why are these competing firms making scotch with a lighter base? The answer is obvious: because they've analysed their own market and discovered where the demand lies.

In order to be successful within any area you enter, you have to study again and again others already successful in that particular area.

Here, then, is our next rule:

Analyse the steps you will have to take within your field in order to reach your goal.

While you are analysing the proper steps, study the easiest possible methods of making them work. Look for opportunities in areas within the same field which you may have missed.

George Axelrod, the playwright, is the author of one of the most successful stage comedies to appear on Broadway, *The Seven Year Itch*. But, as seems to be the case with most people associated with the theatre, the chances of coming up with a Broadway hit are very small compared to the chances of being responsible for a partial success or a failure.

A second play by Axelrod, *Will Success Spoil Rock Hunter?* made money for its author but was hardly in the class of *The Seven Year Itch* as far as its commercial success was concerned. And Axelrod's third play, *Goodbye Charlie*, was unsuccessful.

Now I have no idea what motivated Axelrod to take the direction he did in his career. But it is interesting to observe what happened to it. Suddenly, when one spotted his name in the newspapers, it was no longer in connection with a forthcoming Broadway production. Axelrod had begun concentrating on screenwriting, and later on film production itself. He has since been most successful in this area, having written screenplays for such films as *Bus Stop* and *Breakfast at Tiffany's* and produced and written a number of highly popular movies, including *The Manchurian Candidate* and *How to Murder Your Wife*.

Instead of remaining in one restricted area of show business, which seemed to be showing less chance for reward, Axelrod concentrated on another aspect which promised to be more fulfilling. He has since reaped the rewards of his astute thinking.

Let's take another example—a shoe manufacturer friend of mine, whose first venture happened to be a big success. When he was a beginner, this man had the good fortune of meeting up with one of the most brilliant businessmen in this field. My friend, who was then quite young, listened carefully to the older, more experienced man. The business genius liked the basic idea behind my friend's business plans and decided to collaborate with the young man in setting up a factory. The result was what every businessman dreams about. Not only was the venture enormously successful, but created, in addition to the financial reward, wonderful comments along Wall Street.

It all appeared so simple that after this first venture the young man decided to drop collaboration. He opened a factory of his own, and principally because he had established such an excellent reputation for himself, there was no difficulty in raising money for it. But his product had no consumer acceptance and he eventually went bankrupt.

Undiscouraged, he tried a third venture, and then a fourth. Each ended in disaster.

Now, perhaps this man has made up his mind that he wants to be a success entirely on his own. It would be presumptuous of me to advise him to do otherwise. But it is clear, too, that he is struggling in an area that promises to prove frustrating. His collaboration with the brilliant businessman was an ideal combination, but to him it looked too easy. By choosing the more challenging path, he was faced with repeated failure.

The rule represented by these examples is a very comprehensive one:

Follow the path of least resistance.

Before you do anything, however, you must follow our next, vitally important rule:

Develop patience.

In 1949, the famous multi-millionaire J. Paul Getty bought a tract of land in Saudi Arabia. Despite the fact that oil had not at the time been discovered on the land, he offered a considerable amount in cash, plus a minimum royalty of $1,000,000 a year for it. His purchase of the property was based on detailed information he had received about it.

Mr. Getty received no income from this land for four years, but in May, 1953, a rich strike of oil was finally made in the area. The output of this new field resulted in his becoming the largest independent oil producer in the Middle East and one of the richest men in the world.

The moral? Well, there are several. For one thing, Mr. Getty, as has been noted, explored his particular field thoroughly. He did this by securing information before the purchase. But even more important—and this brings us to our rule—he was patient enough to realize that though there would be no immediate returns on his investment, he would ultimately be making that investment pay off and, what's more, in extraordinary fashion.

In a smaller way, this can happen in any field.

Early in my dancing career, I could have been booked at the Bal Tabarin in Paris. But I knew I was not yet ready for the big time. I wanted to wait—that is, until the time I could appear at that night club as a star, not merely as a featured performer. The chance finally came again two years later, and during those two years I performed at numerous second-rate clubs, receiving a salary that was barely one-fourth of what I might have made at the Bal Tabarin. But by the time the second chance came, I had enough experience to be a headliner. The gamble eventually brought me to my goal: the world fame I coveted so badly.

Some time ago, a friend of mine asked my advice about whether he should accept a partnership in lieu of salary in a newly formed company. The partnership would have provided him with 20 per cent of the profits.

There was every indication in the world that, before very long, the company would be enormously successful, and I insisted that my friend accept, for he had saved sufficient money to live on for at least two years while waiting for the firm to grow. At the end of those two years, his 20 per cent would be worth several hundred thousand dollars, as opposed to the five hundred dollars a week he would be receiving as salary.

Unfortunately, my friend did not take my advice. Today, his salary has been moderately increased, but it is nowhere near the level of income he might have received had he decided to wait.

There is an old saying that even a clock which stands still is right twice a day. In everyone's life there are chances for success, but one has to wait for them.

On the stock market there are specific times when a stock must be bought. If you hope to be a success in the stock market at all, you must recognize these moments and, above all, you must make up your mind when you will have to wait for them. Impetuous buying on the market is invariably the quick path to ruin.

If a wave of hysteria sweeps the country because of a threatened national crisis, you must be smart enough to recognize that the reaction is purely emotional. The drop in the market is temporary and will be lifted once the threat of the crisis vanishes. I know some people who wait for the world to be threatened with war before they will buy stocks. This is surely what one might consider *cynical* buying, but it is also very practical—and it is profitable.

Let's suppose you want to become head of your firm.

It is necessary for you to know exactly who are the people ahead of you on the waiting list. You must know how long it will take you to reach the desired spot, and you must not mind waiting for the spot to become available. In every field, you will have to wait for the significant opportunity. Before you know it, it will be available.

In the first chapter of this book, I discussed the misunderstanding of the word "luck" and how everyone, in the long run, is entitled to luck if he will only recognize it for what it is and help it along when it is thrust upon him.

Actually, there is no such thing as "luck" when you set out to explore the career route you hope to follow. If you patiently hammer away within a particular territory, you will, somehow, create your own favourable circumstances.

During my dancing career, whenever I wanted to appear at a night club in a particular city, I did not write a letter to one club in the hope that it would hire me. I wrote letters to ten clubs, thereby creating greater odds that I would land a job.

By simply increasing your chances for success mathematically, you also increase its probability. You do not have to succeed every time you set out to succeed. Even once may be enough.

People do not remember Verdi for his unsuccessful operas. He is considered great in the opera world because of his successes. Similarly, no one ever mentions the flops of Rodgers and Hammerstein. Most people can't even remember them—and it is just as well.

You have to create your own favourable circumstances, in which "luck" can operate. Sooner or later, "luck" *has* to appear in your life. It is simply impossible to be "unlucky" all the time. If you were always "unlucky" in everything you did you would become a negative genius. Then all you would have to do would be to start doing exactly the opposite of what you want to do.

So let's decide something important: if out of every five efforts you make towards success, *one* turns out right, you can become successful.

A young man is selling a particular magazine and telephones five people every half-hour. He will have made a good deal of money by the end of the day if one out of every five buys a subscription.

Success: Its Best Possible Route

A young lady sends fifty letters to prospective employers. Only five answer and one hires her. Tragic? Nonsense! She just placed herself well ahead of others who are looking for jobs.

The more people to whom the magazine salesman speaks within his allotted time, the greater his chances. The more letters the young lady writes, the greater her opportunity for starting along the road to success.

I am assuming, of course, that you have already analysed yourself sufficiently to know whether you have the talent which you are applying to your particular field. The young lady could send several thousand letters, but if she hasn't the ability, she will soon be fired. But once—through self-analysis as we have discussed it—you recognize where your particular talent lies, make up your mind to increase the number of attempts to gain success.

Let's take an absurd example. Let us suppose your success depends to some extent on having a particular brochure delivered to a client at midnight. The whole trouble, however, is that you are in bed with influenza, a temperature of 102, and there is a blizzard creating havoc in the streets.

Common sense will tell you it is going to be somewhat difficult to persuade a friend to deliver the brochure for you. But you decide to try, anyway. You pick up the telephone and call a friend. He quickly informs you that he would do anything for you—short of delivering a brochure in the middle of the night during a severe blizzard!

You probably expected that reaction. Now try picking up the phone and calling a dozen friends. Make that twenty. If you have no luck persuading any one of the twenty to do this important favour, try phoning forty people you happen to know. Somehow, you will find that at least one person will agree to make that delivery!

67

What you have done is simply to have increased your odds for success. The law of averages has to make things work out that way.

Remember always—set up as many chances for success as possible. Then just wait and see. One of those chances is bound to develop.

Before J. Paul Getty started to drill for oil, he surveyed the territory thoroughly. Since he knew there was oil somewhere on that land and kept drilling, it would have been almost impossible for him to continue and never strike oil.

Practically every successful inventor knows he has to keep submitting his product to a countless number of manufacturers before *one* accepts it. But he also knows that this is part of the game of inventing and that one manufacturer can provide him with a fortune.

If you are applying for a job as a corporation executive, it makes no sense to write one letter to a prospective firm. Write *dozens*. One firm is bound to respond positively.

Our next rule, then, is an all-encompassing one:

Create your own favourable circumstances by increasing your mathematical odds.

As a performer, whenever I visited a new city, I made certain that I had reservations at the most elegant hotel (I was also very budget-conscious, however, and made sure that the room itself was inexpensive). In the long run, the investment paid off, for my act became identified with the image of "class", higher salaries, and bigger billing. Had I lived in squalor I would have been identified accordingly. And in the long run, I would not have become a star performer.

There are many individuals who do not attribute sufficient importance to image-building. Politicians have often failed mainly because of poor images. Barry Goldwater, for example, is probably not half so bad as his image has made some people believe.

The concept of image-building applies just as strongly to the field of business as it does to the entertainment industry or to politics. If a man is identified as a phony, he can never be a respected banker. He may even *be* a phony and get away with it, providing his image makes his business associates believe otherwise.

If you want success, you must decide exactly what your philosophy of life is and build your image around it. If you are an honest man, don't try to be anything else; arrange to make yourself *known* as an honest man.

At least two or three times during my business day I make handshake deals and keep them. Gradually, my reputation for carrying through these handshake deals gets around, and in many cases, my handshake has become as effective as a written contract.

My brother Erno was once operating a successful money-exchange business, and every deal he executed was carried out on his word alone. One day, he concluded a handshake deal which ultimately resulted in his losing forty thousand dollars in a matter of minutes. Nevertheless, he kept his word and made good his losses, though it took him two years to do it. As a result, his reputation spread and his word alone became as effective as a signed contract.

There are no specific rules about what image you should present to others. But you must choose the image that suits you best.

A well-known multi-millionaire is reputed to get away with wearing slippers and a sweater to his business meetings. No one cares, because he and he alone makes all the decisions in his business. But it would be impossible for the president of General Motors to conduct an important board meeting similarly attired.

You will find in life that if you project an image of what you really are, people will generally accept and respect you. Some individuals are desperately afraid of revealing to others their true identities, and, consequently, they present images that are so alien to their personalities that they project themselves as confusing, or, what is worse, dishonest—at any rate, hardly the kind of individual people would be ready to trust.

There is another very important aspect to image-building: tell people about yourself by simply telling them what you do well and what kind of a person you are. Don't be afraid to be honest about yourself even if, at times, you are self-flattering. If you don't believe in yourself, who will?

False modesty has little place in the achievement of success. If you happen to be an expert mountain climber, *tell* someone about it. Let that person tell someone else. Before you know it, the news will come back to you. And the things you say about yourself are always far more effective when someone else repeats them.

In the long run, you are the best promoter of yourself, for there are times when life appears to be one gigantic market in which everyone has to sell himself to others.

You must persuade others of your talent. If you want to be the head of a large organization, you must let them know you are cut out to do the job.

It all boils down to two rules:

Build your image, and

Make your image conform to the person you really are.

As you advance within your particular success area, it is inevitable that you are going to be challenged by others, for these individuals also have success drives. You may even be in for some fairly hectic competition.

It is also possible for you to win that competition if you recognize the other individual's assets and liabilities. You will then understand exactly what you will be up against.

A study of the good attributes and liabilities of your opponent is necessary in whatever field you hope to succeed. You may discover that someone in line for the same promotion as yourself is a man who thrives on intrigue. Once you *recognize* this fact, however, it is a lot easier for you to cope with it.

I know of a rather unfortunate case which occurred recently and concerned a group of people who worked in one of the departments of a large hospital.

The newly appointed director of this department was an energetic young man with more than a fair share of competence in carrying out his duties. The assistant director, however, was an extremely vengeful, aggressive woman who hoped to take over her boss's job herself. Soon things reached the point where she was undermining him at every opportunity. She also decided to see to it that other members of the department were either fired or forced to quit their jobs simply because they supported the director.

One afternoon, the director learned from several close friends at the hospital that his vicious associate had actually set up a secret appointment with the principal director of the hospital. During her discussion with him, the woman had done everything possible to have her boss fired, exaggerating his minor inadequacies and even going so far as to invent major lies along the way. Though the principal director was not entirely convinced the woman was telling the truth, he promised he would watch her boss closely as well as the other members of the department.

When the young director learned about what his assistant had done, he had opportunity to act at once, and it would obviously be the last real chance he had before the woman could carry her scheme to its destructive conclusion.

It would have been wrong to defend himself to the hospital's principal director because no formal charges had been placed against him. His only possible solution was to fire the woman. And if this act happened to be questioned by the principal director, he could have revealed his assistant's easy-to-unravel lying and scheming.

But the course this young man chose was one of *laissez faire*. For one thing, he took pity on the woman, realizing her behaviour for what it was—the actions of a severely emotionally disturbed individual. Instead of protecting himself, he jeopardized his own position and refused to act, deciding to let events take their natural course.

Well, they took their natural course, all right. As a result of his lack of action, not only was the young director eventually fired, but the other members of the department also lost their posts.

As ironic as it may appear, in the long run, this unpleasant woman came off as the only one in the department cut out to be a success. The others—her young boss most of all—failed badly from the standpoint of achieving what they wanted.

Good common sense is an absolute necessity in dealing with others in business. Reactions of an emotional nature have very little place in the competitive world.

Had this particular man been insulted by an irrational stranger on a bus, it would naturally make more sense for him to disregard the stranger's remarks than to try to have the stranger thrown off the bus. But the young man was being attacked by an irrational business associate to such a degree that his success was crippled. He was put in a position where his only weapon was to act. Yet unfortunately he did not.

I do not mean to suggest that ruthlessness is imperative in the business world. But there is one time when you have to be ruthless, and that is when you are about to be destroyed by someone else whose own ruthlessness is quite apparent. Unless you take some strong action against this behaviour, it cannot be stopped. Occasionally, during the course of your career, you will find yourself virtually at war. But you cannot stand by and remain passive.

The failure of Chamberlain in dealing with Hitler over the Czechoslovakian crisis is the most spectacular and disastrous example I can think of in trying to meet ruthlessness with passivity and complacency.

Our rule then is, simply:

Consider the motives of others and act accordingly.

In the Middle Ages, a *Public Success* was a man who mounted a horse and, carrying an enormous lance, did his best to turn himself into a Great Crusader. A stockbroker transformed by H. G. Wells' time machine would have little fun in the fourteenth century.

What I am getting at is a simple concept: When you choose a goal, you have to consider the time and the place where you are trying to achieve that goal. Victor Hugo said: "There is no greater idea than the idea whose time has come."

When asking yourself what it is you want to do, ask yourself, also, is this the right time for someone like me to aim for this particular goal? Am I in the right place?

The important consideration is for you to think of the right moment and the right situation where you can best present yourself.

Most people are at their best at job interviews between the hours of ten thirty and twelve thirty in the morning. They have recovered from the vague fog of the previous night's sleep. And, on the other hand, they are not already worn out by the day's activities. Perhaps it would be a good idea for you to arrange job interviews for yourself within these hours.

There are those who manage to take over large corporations simply because they happen to be at the right place at the right time. But their preparation set them up for the place and the time.

If you wanted to open up a car-rental company, you would obviously not feature a 1931 Packard.

Try to recognize the trend. Know that you have to recognize what people are buying and what is in vogue.

Architects change their styles to fit the popular trend. Fashion houses feature model dresses which they know will appeal to the public's current taste. By the same token, successful people in every field will associate themselves with ideas which are currently in fashion.

Let us suppose you want a job, any kind of a job. Pick up a copy of your local newspaper and recognize which types of job openings are available. The demand is fairly obvious. You will have a much better chance of succeeding in an area where there are the most advertisements than in the area where there are the least. Once you've recognized the trend: act. The time to act is now. If you wait, conditions may change.

Our rule, then, is:

Recognize—through research—the correct time and correct place for your moves.

In analysing your goal, it is not enough to ask yourself

whether there is a need for good people within a particular field. Chances are you will have to pick one or more *specialities* within that field before you can set out to achieve your success.

It is not enough to say, for example, I would like to be a success in sales promotion. What do you want to do in that field? The area of sales promotion has dozens of divisions and subdivisions. Perhaps your talent lies in a merchandising setup. If so, stick to that and that alone. Or perhaps your best area is that of personal contact and you may find it beneficial to pursue job leads which will lead to a position along these lines.

Find out where the needs are within a particular area; see if you have the talent to meet those needs.

The knowledge of one specific area of a particular field is sufficient for you to be successful. If you have capabilities as an electronic engineer, it is much wiser for you to pursue the study of electronic engineering more carefully than it would be for you to attempt to embrace all areas of engineering.

Do not try to know everything.

Medical reporters build extraordinary careers for themselves simply by specializing. Seldom will a medical reporter turn out an article about sports or the law. He will concentrate on medicine alone and, by doing so, will become recognized as the kind of specialist who will undoubtedly be called upon by editors whenever a medical story is needed.

Our rule:

Decide to specialize.

Now we come to our last rule within the area of analysing your situation:

Be ready to compromise.

I have known people so unwilling to make sacrifices of their so-called "principles" that they end up destroying their chances for success.

One should, of course, operate according to a code of behaviour, but it is something else again to get ahead if you are incapable of modifying some of your principles.

You may say to yourself, I am a fine, upstanding Protestant and I will only do business with Protestants. Then along comes a person who is important to your career but happens to be a Catholic. It would be absurd, of course, to reject the business relationship because of the difference in religion.

Everyone who has ever been successful has been willing to "bend" on numerous occasions during the course of his career.

I do not for one moment mean to suggest that you should turn yourself into the veritable "yes man" and jellyfish— this kind of individual is never successful because he is constantly compromising and in actuality is a coward. If you have very strong feelings about something, stand up for them. In the long run, you will achieve more faith in yourself and your own convictions.

I knew a man who walked out of a high-paying job because his boss happened to be, among other things, *unscrupulous*. This man was out of work for several depressing months, but the positive result of his action had such a strong effect on his own personality that his belief in himself developed considerably and he was eventually able to find an even better job than the one he had left.

This man was wisely *unwilling* to compromise his ideals, for integrity was the primary one.

Now let us take a negative example of someone whose list of ideals seems to be headed by *false pride*.

Recently, a friend of mine decided to travel to Brazil,

where he looked up his former brother-in-law. The brother-in-law, a millionaire industrialist, had been an unsatisfactory husband to my friend's sister, but in every other respect, including his over-all integrity, he was quite admirable.

He had remarried and, incidentally, in doing so had remained very friendly and very fair to his former wife.

When my friend visited the industrialist, he was greeted more warmly than he could have imagined. Then came the *pièce de résistance:* the industrialist offered him an extraordinary position with an enormous salary. Even more astounding was the industrialist's offer to pay my friend's living expenses for a period of six months, with the understanding that if he was dissatisfied with his position he could leave it graciously at any time he chose within that period of time.

My friend seemed eager to accept the position. It was a greater opportunity than he had ever dreamed could be offered him in this strange land.

Just at the point when the agreement was about to be settled, however, the industrialist's second wife entered the room. The industrialist introduced her amiably to my friend and the wife extended her hand.

The bitterness my friend had obviously been experiencing over his former brother-in-law's remarriage finally caught up with him. He turned his back on the woman, refusing to take her hand. The end result was predictable: the industrialist was insulted and cancelled the offer. He did not want to be *judged*—and rightly so.

Not only was my friend guilty of false pride, but he was also guilty of illogic. His anger had not been directed against the industrialist for divorcing his sister; it had been directed against the second wife. He obviously could not extricate himself from this absurd emotional reaction—a reaction which *prevented* him from achieving success.

In the business world, it is entirely unnecessary to re-educate others in their religious, political, or moral beliefs. It is also next to impossible. And people will only resent you for it.

The degree of personal compromise varies from goal to goal. An individual who decides to go into the arts may find he has to make his living for a number of years on a job other than the one associated with his goal. The idea is to choose the least painful way of earning money while you are working towards your goal. Sometimes the individual is lucky enough to secure a job in the same field as the one which contains his goal. A young man aiming at a career in advertising, for example, might profitably spend a summer as a door-to-door salesman or as a clerk in a supermarket so as to learn about the consumer market at the grass roots level.

Nearly everything worthwhile in life demands a sacrifice of some sort—at least in the beginning. The man opening up a furniture store might have to keep late hours in order to build up a clientele. The man in love with a particular woman will have to meet at least one or two of her demands which he might feel unreasonable in another woman.

The compromise becomes easy, however, if we recognize the fact that it is an *absolute necessity* as we hit the odd zigzags on our clearly carved route to success.

Here, then, is the list of rules for us to follow when analysing the *best possible route*.

1. Go over in your mind your assets and liabilities as you have learned them through self-analysis.

2. See how these assets and liabilities apply to your particular goal.

3. Analyse thoroughly the field in which you are planning to succeed.

4. Analyse the steps you will have to take within your field in order to reach your goal.

5. Follow the path of least resistance.

6. Develop patience.

7. Create your own favourable circumstances by increasing your mathematical odds.

8. Build your image.

9. Make your image conform to who you really are.

10. Consider the motives of others and act accordingly.

11. Consider the correct time and place for your moves.

12. Decide to specialize.

13. Be ready to compromise.

Let us review briefly the position we have now achieved *en route* to success. We have learned what success means. We have explored ourselves sufficiently to know exactly what kind of success we want. And we have examined the pathway we will be obliged to follow if we are going to make the success dream a reality.

Now the important preparations are over. Our mental luggage has been packed, and we are ready, at last, to embark on the journey itself.

There may, however, be a few shocking surprises along the way.

4 Achieving the Success Goal

BEFORE WE PROCEED ALONG THE SUCCESS ROUTE ITSELF, we must recognize the fact that we are going to have to disregard some of our previous concepts about the business world in general and success in particular.

We must emphasize, once more, that the word "luck" has essentially no meaning in our discussion of success. In place of the word "luck" it would be wise to substitute the less melodramatic word, "opportunity". By doing so, the fantasy of the word "luck" will vanish from our minds.

At various points in our lives, all of us are offered *opportunities*. These are the moments for us to "move in", to prove the fact that we are the ones in command of the situation. But these moments must be recognized and you must take advantage of them.

Another concept we should learn to disregard is our

previous and entirely illogical belief that we must always put the consideration of others before our own "selfish" drives. This is sheer nonsense.

In the history of the world, there has never been a successful person whose actions were motivated just to please the needs of other human beings—unless he profited either emotionally or monetarily by catering to those needs.

Now this may sound like a rather callous summation until you begin thinking about it. I do not wish to imply that we have to step on others or wreak destruction as we climb to the top. No one who has followed this pattern has remained successful very long. There are many notable examples of ruthless individuals who claw their way towards their goals and remain successful for a period of time, but somehow they manage to destroy whatever they happen to have accomplished for themselves.

A person has no right to another's property. Nor does he have the right to hurt others. But the individual *does have the right to put his own needs first.*

Now, the average parent, you say, prides himself on the sacrifices he makes to help his own children. Also, a loving husband will nearly always consider his wife's feelings above his own. And soldiers on a battlefield have been known to have sacrificed their lives for their comrades.

But think about these examples for a moment. Are the motives that create these sacrifices *unselfish?* It would be absurd to think so. We are doing what we want to do simply because of the emotional gratification such sacrifices provide. Love for another human being is, indeed, a noble motive in our lives, but it is also an entirely selfish one. How many parents would sacrifice their lives to help someone else's children? How many husbands would put the feelings of

THE ANATOMY OF SUCCESS

other men's wives before their own personal needs? The answers to these questions are obvious.

One of the most important rules in our battle for success is this:

Develop the power of positive selfishness.

I'll discuss this rule in greater detail a little later on, but I just wanted you to be prepared for it. As cold and as callous as it may sound on a superficial level, in the long run this rule provides ennobling characteristics which we must develop, for through it we can achieve our greatest potential as successful human beings and, above all, human beings of the highest integrity.

Your Plans Are Set, Now Execute Them: The Rules

Once your battle strategy has been set up through analysis of your own personality and the goal you hope to achieve has been set, it is important for you to realize that other individuals are undoubtedly headed in the same direction as yourself, with equally or more effective battle plans. But consider, too, that the individual who has the *superior will-power* will inevitably be the one who wins.

In effect, you are setting out on a race, with other runners starting at the same point as yourself. As the course develops, you will see which runners pull away from the others, which runners fall behind, and which ones drop out altogether. At no moment during this race towards the success goal, no matter how strongly the temptation to do otherwise may strike you, can you vacillate or shrug your shoulders and say to yourself, "Well, I'm not exactly sure I want to continue". Nor can you slow down your pace. If possible, you must turn it into a methodical *gallop*. You must not procrastinate by a day, an hour, or a minute. You must constantly toward the finishing line. Otherwise, you may never make it at all.

You should realize, too, that during the race, a tension has been building up between you and the other runners. The race is gradually developing into a battle of both muscles and mind. Watch the hurdles as they come at you—there will be many. Observe how much easier it is to overcome the second hurdle than it was to jump over the first. See, too, if you are cut out for success, that the third, fourth, and fifth hurdles are even more readily overcome.

But don't let the ease with which you make your progress fool you. There are many more steps the runner must take before he reaches the final point of glory.

As I've mentioned before, life is like a market. But it is also like an athletic field. If you are striving to become leader of a large corporation, there are at least a dozen others who are in the race with you. And you must make sure you are following all the rules, including the easier ones—the ones you may have a tendency to minimize or overlook altogether.

Your determination must be such that you become a veritable *octopus*, with "feelers" working in all directions.

As an aspirant to the position of corporation head, you must explore every area of the business in which you find yourself. Active interest in your corporation's union, for example, may be something for which you have little time and even less interest. What is worse, you might consider such activity insignificant. Yes, it may possibly be insignificant in comparison with the work itself which you are required to perform, but it is most significant in terms of your larger goal. At a crucial point in your career, you could very easily discover that your understanding of union activity is the very thing to provide your advancement.

83

Successful leaders of corporations have been known not only to recognize the executives of their corporation by their first names, but they also know the first names of their clerks and typists.

Then, once more, you have to take into account this problem of "the consideration of others." Let us suppose you have an important business engagement—not an overwhelming one perhaps but important nevertheless. Your wife, however, happens to have a headache and implores you to cancel the appointment and spend the evening at home with her. Although her ailment is slight, you yield to her wish. Directly or indirectly, your cancelling this particular appointment might ultimately cost you your success, for sometimes it takes years before such a mistake catches up with you.

Never for one moment forget the race and the fact that the others are still in the running.

In my career as a dancer, I missed only one performance, and that was because an aeroplane scheduled to fly from London to Paris had been grounded because of bad weather. My determination was so strong, however, that I wanted to charter a plane to take me to France. The cost of this elaborate gesture would have been more than ten times the amount of salary I would have received for the Paris engagement. Yet I was determined to make my show. Unfortunately, this was one of those rare cases in which I was at the mercy of my environment and, my determination notwithstanding, no pilot would make the journey in such poor weather. So, for the first time in my career, I missed a performance.

But there were many, many other occasions when I could readily have excused myself from performances, times when I was ill with high fever and occasions, too, that involved bitter personal tragedy. My determination remained: I had to make the next show.

Most of us are constantly faced with seemingly minor chores which appear easy to disregard. Because he has made a last-minute date with a beautiful woman, an executive decides to cancel his plans to have dinner with an important business associate. The way out is a lot more dangerous than he imagines. All he has to do—he *thinks*—is pick up the telephone and explain apologetically how enervating his day has been. The business associate is sure to understand for he, too, must have gone through similar days. What difference could it possibly make to put off the appointment until the following evening?

Doing something like this is ultimately destructive. Somewhere in the back of this business associate's mind the offence will be felt. The slight remains a small, possibly even unconscious, one. But it is still there. And somewhere along the line, it is going to develop into a cancer. At a future date, a decision may be weighing in the balance, and the twinge of rejection which may have been felt by this associate can cause a negative decision.

One other thing you are doing to yourself by delaying or postponing things you know you must carry out: you are setting yourself up emotionally for eventual failure. The next time, it will be much easier to take the easy way out. In effect, you are conditioning yourself to be undisciplined.

Had my determination weakened to miss a particular dancing engagement, I would have undoubtedly missed a second and then a fifth and a twentieth performance. And my goal for world fame would never have been reached.

Your determination to succeed must be so strong that, unless all hell breaks loose, you keep those engagements, carry out your responsibilities, and continue running that race. You are actually waging *total war*. And you do not want to miss the biggest or the smallest target.

Without this kind of determination, you will *never* achieve the goal you want. You may come near it perhaps; you may experience a mild form of success. But that ultimate goal—the one you have set up for yourself—will belong to someone else.

Our rule—possibly the most difficult one to follow in our striving for success—is:

Make yourself entirely uncompromising in your determination and drive.

And an important subsidiary rule here is:

Do not neglect seemingly small or insignificant matters which pertain to your goal.

Now we come to the rule we have already mentioned. The one which to some people may sound nasty: *Develop the power of positive selfishness.*

If you are the sort of individual who is constantly beleaguered by your concern for other people's desires and hopes, you are not really cut out for success. But what is worse, you are actually not fulfilling your role as a worthwhile human being.

If you constantly put the consideration of others before what will unquestionably be best for yourself, you are turning yourself into a slave of others, for in a sense, you are working for them. You may even end up making *them* achieve their particular goals. But you will *never* realize your own.

I recently attended a cocktail party where I struck up a conversation with a rather talented but unproduced playwright. His work had been considered, from time to time,

86

for off-Broadway production, but at the moment he remained unrecognized by the general public.

In the past I had read a number of this young man's scripts and thought they had considerable merit. Therefore, it puzzled me that none of his work had been performed in a professional theatre. I asked him how he was getting along with his writing, and he told me the following story which, I must admit, upset me a great deal.

The playwright had a good friend who, like himself, was unrecognized, a young man whom he described as having great potential as a stage director. This friend had assisted him quite a bit on the writing of his latest script. He had done so, not with any promise of reward in mind, but merely as a gesture of friendship and because he was sincerely interested in the playwright's work.

Along came a well-known off-Broadway producer who read the script and loved it. He phoned the playwright almost immediately after he finished reading the play and said he wanted to produce it in a respectable off-Broadway theatre and with an outstanding leading actor. The producer was sure the play would be a hit and make a name for the struggling writer.

But the playwright just as quickly informed the producer that he felt himself obligated to his friend, the aspiring director, for helping him with the play and that under no circumstances would he permit the play to be done unless his friend directed it. After all, the playwright pointed out, if it hadn't been for his friend, the script would not be in such excellent shape.

Well, one can judge a playwright's work simply by looking at the things he writes. But how is it possible to judge the work of an unknown director unless one has seen a performance he has directed? Therefore, never having seen the work of the playwright's friend, the producer very sensibly refused to go along with the suggestion. Besides, the producer pointed out, he had a far more experienced director in mind for the play, someone who could practically assure its success.

Nevertheless, the playwright offered a flat "no", and when the producer said he would send back the script, the playwright felt immensely proud of himself for standing up for his "moral obligation".

After the playwright finished telling me his story, he was a little surprised to find me wincing. I found nothing particularly admirable about what the young man had done. For one thing, he had accomplished nothing in the way of furthering his career and may have even hampered it a little by revealing his own naïveté to an experienced producer. But—and this he hadn't considered—he was possibly hurting his friend, the director, for both men remained undiscovered after the playwright's script was rejected. On the other hand, had the playwright agreed to the producer's terms, he might have created a big enough name for himself to be able to insist on his own director for his second play. Also, he was sure to have made important contacts through the production of his first play, contacts who could have undoubtedly helped not not only his own career but the career of his director friend as well. But because of his misconception of moral obligations, nothing was gained.

Returning to our analogy between life and an athletic field a moment, imagine the following situation: During the race one of the runners injures his knee, and a second runner pauses to help him.

Sound absurd? Of course it is. But it is no less absurd than the manner in which the young playwright behaved. If the second runner was so intent on helping, his best bet would have been to win the race *first* and help the other runner *afterwards*. And chances are he would have done a better job of it!

But now let's take a contrasting example by altering the story of the young playwright. Let us suppose the director and the playwright had made a *definite pact* before beginning work on the script: the director was to offer his services in exchange for which the playwright could not permit the work to be performed without his friend directing it.

Now this has nothing to do with moral obligations or ideals; this is a binding agreement between two parties.

It goes without saying that the playwright would have had to say "no" to a production unless his friend were hired. If he did not stick to this agreement, his action would have been dishonest and, in the long run, bound to cause him serious trouble in or out of the law courts.

The difference in the two examples is that, in the real-life case, the consideration of the playwright was illogical and ultimately destructive. In the fabricated example, by insisting his friend be hired for the job, the playwright was merely carrying out a legitimate business deal.

It must be clearly understood that the road to success cannot be travelled without using other people. You must maintain one moral trait, and that is to avoid deliberately harming other individuals. But you must also be able to *use* people to your own advantage without harming them. And you *must compensate* for using them, for if you do not, you ultimately will lose self-respect.

When a man stands for public office he is, in a sense, using the people who vote for him. He will use their emotions, appeal to what *they* want to hear him say, and yet he must also remain honourable and a good candidate. And when elected, he must *serve well*.

While you are learning to use others without harming them, it is even more important for you not to be used by others who insist on harming *you*.

The chairman of a very large company once presented a tentative offer to a friend of mine, promising to hire him to head one of the industrialist's projected enterprises. My friend, a retired and greatly respected executive, felt he would be unable to remain idle very long and reacted enthusiastically. In the days following the tentative offer, however, whenever he called the industrialist at his office, the latter would refuse to commit himself one way or the other. Nevertheless, he insisted my friend wait until the decision was made.

Finally, my friend realized *he* was the one who had to make the decision. And the decision had to be based on reality! The industrialist had offered him nothing in the way of a contract or even a verbal agreement. It was obvious that he was merely stalling. Perhaps the industrialist took sadistic delight in behaving in this manner, or perhaps he had *never* intended to engage him. In any case, my friend knew he couldn't wait for the industrialist to make up his mind and began looking for another job just as if the industrialist had never made his initial offer.

Later, and much to his surprise, my friend discovered that the industrialist had merely been using his name as an incentive to persuade young, promising executives to work for him.

Here again, our old enemy "consideration of others" pops up and possibly does so under the deceptive guise of "good will".

Another man might have said to himself the following: "Well, this chairman is friendly enough to me. And why would he even bother bringing up the matter unless he intended to engage me? I'll just wait a while. He's sure to come through."

Such thinking, needless to say, is an almost certain path to self-destruction.

One other interesting point might be indicated here. If you sense someone is using you in a negative manner, here is your chance to *use* him right back—and turn this justifiable action into a capital gain.

While the industrialist pretended he was going to hire my friend for his enterprise, my friend decided to go along with this pretence in so far as other enterprises were concerned. He told the heads of these enterprises about the industrialist's offer. He told them that the industrialist wanted him to come out from retirement, his age notwithstanding. This reverse action on his part worked beautifully. The chairmen of a number of top-notch firms found themselves carried away with interest, and my friend ended up with an even greater position than the one tentatively offered by the industrialist.

In trying to avoid being exploited by others, you should also differentiate between being truly exploited and being used in a manner which will help you achieve your goal.

I think the following example will explain what I mean:

A young man has just got his degree in law and has the excellent fortune of landing a job with a top firm. Predictably, his salary is quite low and his hours, also predictably, are long. But what the young man has not counted on is the insufferable nonsense he has to put up with in the office itself.

For one thing, nearly every top lawyer of the firm insists on making the young man spend an inordinate amount of time checking through old briefs for information applicable to current cases. And, what is even more irritating, whenever an important client calls at the office, the young graduate is made to serve as little more than a glorified office boy.

Is this young man being exploited? Of course not! He is merely doing what nearly every young man has done upon graduation. He is working, not so much for salary or dignity, but for experience. His goal, we assume, is to become a successful lawyer, and while he is gaining experience, it is a small price for him to put up with a few inconveniences that may occur.

Now, let us take another example:

Five years go by. The young man has proved his worth admirably. He has already helped to prepare quite a number of very successful cases. He decides to switch jobs—and now he finds himself at another large law firm, where he hopes to work full time on his blossoming career, but he is made, once again, to function in his dual capacity.

Is he being exploited *now?* The answer should appear obvious. The best thing he could do at this point in his career is look for another job.

At the beginning of my dancing career, there were many occasions when I was obliged to help build scenery in night clubs. I did it cheerfully because I knew I was, ever so indirectly, helping to achieve my ultimate goal. As my career progressed, wasting my time in this way would naturally have proved demeaning.

Remember that, though it is important for you to manifest a certain amount of ego-strength while you strive for success, you should not become confused between "ego-strength" and "false pride". The moment you take your eyes away from your *ultimate goal* and concentrate on the insignificant hurts or slights you have received, you are in for trouble.

When I began my career as a writer and editor of crossword puzzles in Hungary, the publisher of the newspaper for which I worked would often send me fifteen miles back to my house to make a minor correction in my copy. In the beginning, I felt deeply wounded, but soon I began to consider it was only the start of my career and the publisher was providing me with valuable experience. When I had sufficient experience to take my work to another publisher, I did exactly that. Catering to this publisher's idiosyncrasies was no longer necessary to achieve my particular goal at that time.

Our rules, concerning when and if we should let ourselves be used by others, may be summed up as follows:

Do not let yourself be used by others unless they are directly helping you achieve your goal.

Do not let false pride hinder the achievement of your goal.

Decision-Making—How Does It Serve Your Goal?

One of the foundations of success—and also one of the most difficult to build—is the quality of decision-making.

It is particularly difficult to make decisions when three or four alternatives present themselves. Nothing is clear-cut. Everything has its black, white, and grey sides. Sometimes the ambivalence of a particular situation will tend to confuse us to the point where we become easily swayed in a certain direction for reasons that aren't as significant as we imagine them to be.

I think one of the major problems we encounter in making any kind of decision is our basic conflict between what we *know intellectually* to be true and what our *emotions tell us.* Intuition is a very important characteristic of the successful person, but the reason that intuition in such a person comes off as positive is that it is based almost entirely on a subconscious assimilation of *real facts* and an analysis of them.

Let us take, as an example, a case I happened to hear about recently. A fairly prominent businessman made an error of judgement—based solely on his own highly emotional overreaction to an individual—which nearly resulted in destroying his company.

The company had been faltering badly in recent years and was at the point of folding entirely when its board of directors was presented with a fortunate opportunity. The chairman of another and far more successful organization proposed a merger. It was a merger which had every indication of rescuing the faltering company in the nick of time.

One of the weak company's leading executives—the individual who is the principal subject of this little story —arranged a meeting with the chairman of the other company to discuss initial plans for the merger. Everything had been progressing reasonably well until that first meeting.

But the moment they encountered one another, their two personalities clashed. The successful company chairman struck the other as agressively self-assertive, a characteristic which had a particularly unnerving effect on the troubled executive. Somehow, once the man recognized this personality trait in the other, nothing the latter had to offer seemed quite right. By the end of the meeting, the troubled executive was filled with feelings of hopelessness and the threat of ultimate dissension.

The following morning, without giving sufficient time to an analysis of his emotional reaction, he typed a lengthy report to the board of directors of his firm, insisting that the merger be given a great deal of additional consideration. The tone of the report was completely negative and contained one or two absurd references to the possibility of a merger with other firms, firms the executive should have realized would never possibly take on the burdens of the faltering company.

Needless to say, the board of directors gave the executive's report a good deal of attention. There was even a time when it looked as if the merger would fall through entirely, for there ensued a series of totally unnecessary phone calls and meetings which the faltering company initiated merely to confirm their chairman's report. The successful company was antagonized by these proceedings, and its chairman threatened to join hands with another corporation. Fortunately, other executives at the faltering company came to the rescue and managed to effect the merger.

Today, the joint company is extraordinarily successful, and somehow the troubled executive's fears and doubts simply never materialized.

What really initiated his decision to write that destructive memo, one so dangerous that it might have wrecked whatever remained of his organization?

The executive was upset by a personality trait of the successful company's head—a trait which, he should have recognized, had *always* jolted him in other people, regardless of who they happened to be. Knowing this fact about himself, he should have made a strong attempt to clear his prejudice from his mind. He should have realized that it mattered little whether he *personally liked* this other man. But his reaction was entirely lacking in an intellectual approach to the situation, for the chairman of the successful company had already proved that his business ideas worked most effectively.

Often, however, making wrong decisions is not so harmful as making no decisions at all. Wavering back and forth is what is really disastrous.

The successful person's most striking characteristic is that he is capable of making a decision at exactly those moments when decision-making is necessary. And once that decision is made, he must stick to it.

For those who have difficulties making decisions, may I

suggest one important consideration to follow: *Would your decision help you achieve your particular goal?*

In the case of the troubled executive, his goal was inextricably tied up with the goal of his company: both the executive and the company were interested in being successful. Therefore, he should have recognized that a personality trait like brashness on the part of the company chairman had little or no bearing on whether a merger between the two firms could prove fruitful. He had not even bothered to consider the important facts.

When making decisions, always keep your goal in mind. Consider always how the decision will affect your goal. Remember: *the achievement of the goal is of paramount importance.*

There may be moments when you arrive at the meeting of a number of roads and will have to decide which is the more profitable one to follow. It may be a question of taking the superhighway or the short cut. Before deciding which road to follow, you must balance the pros and cons. For instance, the short cut is *short* but it may also be a precarious road to follow, while the superhighway is long but offers definite assurance of getting where you want to go. Consider whether it is worth the risk to take the shorter route, which may prove only to be a dead end.

Our rules then, on decision-making, are:

Base your decisions on intellectual—never emotional —*considerations.*

Consider always how these decisions will help you achieve your ultimate goal.

Balance the odds when you decide upon a particular direction.

There is still another rule concerning decision-making, and I think it should be listed separately. It is simply:

Watch for unforeseen dangers.

Achieving the Success Goal

When you make a decision in relation to your success goal, you must be very aware of the odd little unforeseen occurrences that disturb, and sometimes disrupt, your journey.

A great many failures come about because the person engaged in the success struggle continues to concentrate solely upon the trip itself and fails to examine the possibilities of what may happen on the road. Consider as an example the individual who decides to make a great deal of money on the stock market and knows nothing about the stock he is buying other than that it has been offered as a "hot tip" by a broker or possibly someone of less authority.

Very often, big losses on the market occur in exactly this manner, and they are tragic to behold. This type of speculator usually does nothing to consider the possibilities of his stock plunging downward. He is unprepared for a negative outcome. The tipster has told him the stock is "hot", but the investor does not look out for dangers which may arise. Therefore, he is unable to cope with a possible drop in the market if it should occur.

When someone stands for political office, he must consider another kind of danger: will he be prepared to accept another role in society if he is not elected? If he loses the election and has not considered what new and satisfying role he can follow, his spirit will be completely broken. If, however, he enters the political race with the knowledge that it is possible for him to suffer defeat, he will have made adequate preparations for a rewarding life in the event of failure. He may even, if he is clever enough, make capital out of his defeat.

There is a recent case of a beautiful queen of an Asian country whose divorce resulted in the loss of her noble title and who was subsequently banned from the aristocratic society in which she was accustomed to spend her time. Wisely, this lovely and clever young woman made capital of her former title by becoming a film actress. Here, within an entirely different society, she is now able to lead a complete and rewarding life.

There are so many cases of famous personalities who have ultimately turned their defeats and sufferings into gains that it would be superfluous to mention them. Dangers to their careers were suffered by all of them, but what they did with these problems actually helped their careers.

Consider the worst that can happen to you if you follow a particular road. Assume, for a moment, that it *will* happen to you and decide what turn your life will take if it does. If the possibility of such a development appears too painful, don't even risk travelling along that road.

I mentioned in the previous chapter my decision to risk a lot of money to sponsor a fashion show. In effect, I was investing this amount of money as insurance against losing the sum it would have cost to buy the fashion house itself. In this particular case, gambling with a smaller stake appeared reasonable, and I therefore proceeded with my calculated risk.

If you find, while travelling along your particular route—be it short cut or superhighway—that you have unfortunately taken a futile pathway, you must have enough courage and wisdom to return once more to your starting-point. Perhaps you will have to go back even farther, pausing to analyse your assets and liabilities once again to see exactly where that big error in judgment was made. Maybe your goal was poorly chosen. Perhaps you should be directing yourself towards a variation of the same goal. In any case, you know you must go back and re-evaluate yourself and your situation and start with a clean slate. There are sure to be other goals at that beginning point that will look appealing to you.

Conventional Rules—Can You Make Them Work For You?

Anyone who has had a share of success, no matter how small that success has been, must surely have come to an important conclusion: that he has paid little if any attention to the rules which govern the average individual.

Conventional sets of rules are devised for conventional sets of people, people who never rise above the level of mediocrity in their careers or professions. We have already explored the fallacy of constantly putting the needs of other human beings before our own needs. We have seen, too, where such thinking tends to lead us.

A conventional individual would not think in terms of losing money before making it. Some of the shrewdest people I know take three or four calculated business risks simultaneously, *knowing* they will lose money with all but one of these investments. The single business venture, however, could provide them with far more profit than all their investments combined. Thus, the fact that they lose money matters very little.

Yet, there are very few people who think in these terms. The conventional individual will guard his capital jealously, afraid to make a move unless he feels he is assured a definite profit from every single investment.

In order to be successful, one has to be *different*. A *different* style of doing things, perhaps. A *different* approach to business problems. A *different* method of promotion.

Consider, too, the appeal and promotion value of a new product or an original idea. There may be numerous imitations of them, but the originals were the first and so they rank supreme, at least for a while.

The famous fashion house of Schiaparelli created a name for itself in the 1920s because it introduced offbeat styling. Similar examples are to be found in other businesses.

In whatever field you hope to achieve recognition, whatever career or job you have set up for yourself, keep in mind that you must produce at least one creation which will stand out by itself as *original* and *unconventional* for what it is. Successful architects have made names for themselves in exactly this manner. Composers have evolved styles of their own which have lent excitement to their work and have made it more and more acceptable as each work appeared. Prominent businessmen have produced new and exciting methods of furthering the progress of their firms.

Our rule is:

Find unconventional patterns.

When Is Your Moment—Do You Recognize It?

As I have stated earlier, there is no person whose opportunities in life simply do not come. The only trouble is that the unsuccessful person does not see them.

If life is like a wheel and the thing we call "opportunity" a mere point on that wheel, we realize that we must reach out and grab that point at the right moment without hesitation. These are the moments when achieving success is easiest. If we hesitate too long, we have to wait for the wheel to revolve again.

A perfect example of this grasping onto the right thing at the right moment may be found, once again, in stock-market dealings. Here, if you do not act on a certain day, or even at a certain hour, the next hour or day may be too late.

A young lady once asked my advice about a tip she had received to invest some money in some Canadian mining stock. She wanted to know what I thought about such an investment. I promptly asked the young lady if she had bought the stock. She said she had not. I then asked her when she had heard about the stock. "About a week ago," she replied.

The solution to her problem was apparent to me, immediately; she should forget she had ever heard the tip. If the tip had had any merit at all—and only one out of ten tips of this type have any real merit—it was now too late for her to buy. The stock had probably already made its upward move.

I once had an idea of producing a play that was a kind of courtroom drama based on the trials of Oscar Wilde. As I negotiated with others on this project, the opportunity for another theatrical venture arose and I temporarily set aside my plans. By the time I was ready to return to the Wilde play, two British films, released simultaneously in this country, concerned themselves with basically the same subject matter. Though the idea of shelving my project hurt me emotionally, I knew that now the play would have little chance of commercial success. I hadn't acted quickly enough and had to suffer for it.

We seem to be at the beginning of a film era in which the James Bond type of tongue-in-cheek suspense melodrama is highest in popularity. Wise film producers are hopping on the bandwagon and taking advantage of this new trend. By acting now, they are making money. But if they were to make long-range plans for a James Bond type movie to be produced five or ten years from now, there is no guarantee that their film would achieve any degree of significant success.

Remember, if you happen to be successful within a

particular field and happen to recognize the beginning of a trend in that field, act quickly, for, before very long, more and more people will be responding to the same trend, and the trend will ultimately lose its novel appeal and possibly disappear entirely.

Our next rule then, as you have probably surmised, is merely:

Act quickly.

A man who, at one time, had been a very promising businessman had dinner with me recently and discussed in detail the terrible error he had made in leaving the job where he had been so lauded by his firm and where he had made a great deal of money. Inexplicably, he had quit his job to try something new—to take a position with another firm in an entirely different field from the one in which he had been working.

I asked him bluntly why on earth he had left his previous job to go to work at a job which, at best, put him in a precarious situation. His answer was confusing, but I had heard this type of answer before, from other individuals: he simply *did not know why.*

Unfortunately, his answer is typical of self-destructive people.

Did the man like his previous job? Very much so. Did he feel he was making a sufficient salary? More than sufficient. There was no reason, at least on a conscious level, for him to leave his winning spot.

I know of many cases like this. In one particular case, a young man was on the road to becoming one of the great successes in the paper industry. He built a thriving business in the matter of two years, and there was every indication that his company would become a major firm in the industry.

An impressive article on the young man and his firm had even appeared in *Fortune*.

Only a few weeks after the *Fortune* article appeared and the industry itself took notice of his firm, I saw a newspaper item stating that the businessman had decided to give up his plans temporarily and sign a deal with a European automobile firm which he would represent in the United States.

About twelve months passed. The automobile venture apparently provided little reward, either in prestige or financial returns, and the young man did everything in the world to get back into his former field. But now he was out of touch with the paper industry. In fact, in the industry, his name was practically forgotten.

I will not presume to say that the young man had not been sincere and well meaning in changing fields. But I must add that he had obviously not given his own career route sufficient thought. He hadn't really "made it" to the point where he could afford to give up one field and branch out in an entirely different one. Had he stayed with his career in the paper industry, as it rose to what looked like supreme success, he might eventually have been able to devote more time to other ventures and become successful in several fields.

But he left his career at the worst possible moment. Ultimately, he gained nothing.

Therefore, once you have recognized a particular trend and have begun to follow it, there isn't a reason in the world for you to look around and try to follow other trends. You must apply what is our next rule:

Stay with the winner.

Here, then, is our complete list of rules for achieving the success goal.

1. Develop the power of positive selfishness.
2. Make yourself entirely uncompromising in your determination and drive.
3. Do not neglect seemingly small or insignificant matters which pertain to your goal.
4. Do not let yourself be used by others unless they are directly helping you achieve your goal.
5. Do not let false pride hinder the achievement of your goal.
6. Base your decisions on intellectual—never emotional —considerations.
7. Consider always how these decisions will help you achieve your ultimate goal.
8. Balance the odds when you decide upon a particular direction.
9. Watch for unforeseen dangers.
10. Find unconventional patterns.
11. Act quickly.
12. Stay with the winner.

We have reached the point in this book where we have examined *how to achieve success*. Now we want to explore the things we should do *once success has been achieved*.

It is a most crucial area of our discussion. If we happen to make a chance error as we proceed along our success route, what we lose is relatively easy to recoup. But one uncorrected error made after the goal has been achieved can ruin us forever.

Consider the point you have reached. Now that you have achieved your success goal, you have entered an entirely different world. While inwardly you may have remained the same individual, you have undoubtedly achieved greater assurance. This assurance will help you achieve even more than you have now. But don't let it mislead you.

The mere state of "being successful" demands that certain of your behaviour patterns change. You may even find yourself developing an entirely new and vibrant philosophy on how to conduct your career—and, possibly, your life in general.

PART TWO

SUCCESS

Protecting It

5 Making Success Permanent

A MAN I MET IN EUROPE ABOUT TEN YEARS AGO—AND WITH whom I have kept in occasional contact—telephoned me one afternoon and said he wanted to meet for drinks to discuss some extraordinary good fortune which had befallen him. He had apparently just made an excellent coup, having taken over a large and very lucrative plastics corporation. Never before in his life had he been in such an eminent position.

It is seldom that I have heard a voice on the telephone pitched to so high a key of elation. His state of bliss was overwhelming; he could barely get through a sentence without laughing uproariously from sheer delight at his triumph.

Now I had always recognized this man as a hard-working, ambitious businessman, determined more than most people to achieve success. And I was certainly pleased with the good fortune he spoke about on the phone. But I must admit, even then, I was vaguely apprehensive that something in his attitude had changed.

When we met several days later, my suspicions were confirmed. The man appeared half-mad with ecstasy. In fact, it was almost impossible to communicate with him, for whenever I made an even remotely practical reference to his newly discovered success, he burst right in with a stream of self-flattery, reminding me again and again of what he had just accomplished.

It wasn't his immodesty which upset me. It was simply that I knew he was heading for trouble.

At one point, I managed to interrupt his exuberance with a few suggestions as to what he could now do to build up his business even further. I didn't want to sound preachy—and I probably would not have offered even a minor bit of advice had I not sensed the danger he was bound to encounter before very long. I had seen others in a similar situation, people who had won significant victories in their success struggle but who, unfortunately, were so carried away by their achievements, that to *hold on to* these achievements seemed relatively easy. They had been misled into thinking that they had reached the point where they could relax. They had worked hard and long for their successes so that now they could sit back and enjoy what was coming to them.

What this type of individual does not realize is that the moment he has achieved his goal is the *worst possible time* to "relax".

Several months passed after my meeting over cocktails, when I heard from a mutual acquaintance that the new company chairman had just embarked on a five-week holiday cruise, leaving the company in the hands of a few office managers. A number of brightly cheerful picture post-cards, sent to me from an assortment of tropical resorts, confirmed this bit of information.

After my friend returned from his trip, well-tanned and relaxed enough to settle down, the self-indulgence took an even more startling turn for the worse. Whatever business sense he had possessed seemed to have vanished entirely. In the months that followed, I learned of foolish decisions, shocking investments and once, in a trade publication, I read about an absurd plan which his company was financing to bring an absolutely worthless product to the market.

This time, I was the one who initiated a meeting with him. Once again, we discussed his business. There was a mild but noticeable change in him since our previous get-together. He had mellowed somewhat and was less involved with his fantasies; yet, even so, the fact that he had made a success of himself still appeared far more important than *holding on* to that success. Again, he told of the remarkable feats he had carried out to achieve his position.

Suddenly and unexpectedly, I lost my temper. I said I recognized that he had accomplished a great deal and had been most shrewd in becoming chairman of such an impressive firm. But what had he done *since* the appointment? Where was he leading his firm, *now*? Every move he made, every attitude he maintained, I pointed out, was clouded by fantasy, by a dream-world image which came from basking in his own glory. If he didn't get back to the realities of his situation soon, he was destined for the destruction not only of himself but of his entire firm as well!

As I anticipated, my advice did nothing more than turn my friend temporarily against me. He flew into a rage and stormed out of the restaurant where we were having dinner.

It was exactly two weeks later that I received an urgent, almost hysterical, phone call from this man. He had just checked over his books very carefully, he told me, and had discovered much to his horror that I had been quite right: the firm's financial standing was steadily on the decline! Also, he had initiated a thoroughly detailed research into the marketability of the new product he hoped to manufacture and had discovered the chances of selling his product on a large-scale basis were next to impossible.

For the first time since his success, my friend was involved in some very real considerations of how to make his company work. He wanted to know any ideas I might have to help the firm recover from its financial slump and prevent it from falling apart altogether. Some of the ideas he himself had developed in the past few days seemed sound enough to me. At least they were worth trying, for they were based on intellectual considerations rather than dreams.

By the time of this writing, I'm glad to say, my friend's corporation is back on its feet again. I don't think its chairman will be in any great hurry to go off into a dream world again (unless, of course, he is absolutely certain the company can operate efficiently without his guidance). Now, even bigger things are anticipated for this firm.

That my friend regained his emotional control in time is a tribute not only to his innate business sense but to the fact that he is essentially a *successful* person, that he is aware, at least now, that success can be lost far more readily than it can be achieved. We have seen as we've completed each of the basic steps in achieving the success goal—to analyse yourself, to choose a goal, and to proceed along the best possible route—that it is imperative that a series of rules be followed. It is no less imperative that you abide by a set of definite rules once your success goal has been accomplished. Our first rule on protecting the success we have achieved is simply:

Keep up your drive.

Keeping up one's drive is comparable with keeping vigilance on the security of one's country. The greatest danger facing the individual—and one which seems to cause the largest number of dropouts in the success game—is the temptation to relax this drive, to feel that, since you have accomplished so much, you can really enjoy your success by doing *absolutely nothing.* I consider this attitude pretty much the same thing as, let's say, the United States taking its Polaris submarine off its twenty-four-hour alert simply because the world has grown relatively peaceful.

The most successful company heads are those who never relax their drive or abandon their "twenty-four-hour alert." They are forever interested in new ideas, new products, and continued growth of their organizations based on investments in research which they know, somehow, will ultimately pay off. They realize, too, that sometimes the most seemingly unpromising products can contain extraordinary chances for success. At least, they take the time and make the effort to examine such products.

Recently, I was approached by an inventor of a process designed to preserve fresh flowers for a period of at least a year. When the inventor explained how the process worked and showed me the result of some of his labours, I knew at once that the product was hardly what one might call "perfected". Yet, I became extremely intrigued with the idea and showed the preserved flowers to a number of other businessmen on the chance that they might be as interested as I was in investing money in developing the process further.

I was amazed at some of their reactions. A few scoffed at

the whole concept and said the flowers I showed them looked no more real than the artificial flowers they had seen in the stores. Others surprised me even more by asking why the inventor had bothered preserving dandelions when preserved orchids would obviously have been so much more desirable.

I couldn't understand their negative attitudes. It was as if they had entered a florist's shop and were considering buying the flowers to take home to their wives. No one was asking them to fall in love with the bunch of flowers I held before them; no one was even asking them to buy them. I was merely inquiring what they thought of the whole concept.

Some time afterwards, I realized what the trouble was. These businessmen had merely seen *the flowers*. Nothing more.

When I was initially presented with this idea, I must immodestly admit I considered more important matters. For one thing, I asked myself, "What is the future of this process?" And for another, "What is the future of the inventor himself?" The flowers mattered little. Naturally they were in an imperfect state. But I asked myself (a) was the general idea a good one? and (b) what could this inventor possibly develop *two years from now?* These were the considerations which seemed to matter to me more than anything else. Also, if the answers to these questions were positive, maybe it would pay just to finance the inventor's *future research.*

I was recently involved in another incident concerning a new invention. A European businessman asked what I thought of the idea of investing money in the production of an automatic machine which uses fingerprints as an identifying device on accident-insurance forms. The process had already been used quite successfully at Austrian ski resorts.

The machine works basically in this manner: instead of bothering to fill out lengthy forms before the skier insures himself, he merely places his fingerprints on a special form which is subsequently put into a machine. The form is later referred to in the event of the skier is injured, with his own fingerprints serving as a kind of identification. The European businessman was attempting to raise the capital to promote the machine in various ski resorts in the U.S. and other countries in the world which were, as yet, unfamiliar with it.

Immediately, I thought, "Why does this machine have to be used only in ski resorts? Why not in other areas where this type of accident insurance could apply?" It amazed me that those already associated with the production of these machines had not explored its numerous possibilities.

Once you're successful, you have to keep your mind open to as many paths and possibilities as are within your reach. You may even discover a field entirely unrelated to what you are doing. But follow all new directions, for they will keep you awake and revitalize you. In some cases they will even galvanize you into a definite action. The danger in not keeping your mind open to new ideas is that you may eventually grow stale.

Sometimes, it's even necessary to leave your field temporarily so that when you return to it you can do so with the proper perspective.

I know, for example, the head of a large electronics firm who is now devoting nearly all of his energies and interests to the possibilities of producing office equipment on a large scale. The electronics side of his firm has been safely taken care of, for that company head has made certain that experts are in charge, and the output of electronic devices is greater than ever. But now the company head feels the time has come for him to explore other areas of industry and then relate what he learns in those fields to his own.

When I became interested in the flower industry, I found this interest aided me a great deal in the fashion field, an area in which I had already achieved some success. I realized, for example, that by exploring problems in marketing large quantities of flowers I was indirectly learning about the problems that arose in marketing certain types of fashion items. Both products were subject to the aesthetic taste of a large segment of the population.

The important thing is to keep your mind open to new ideas and other pathways than the one you're presently following.

The second of our rules in maintaining success is: *Follow new directions.*

Now let's examine what a third rule has in store for us: *Watch out for competition which may threaten your success.*

Now that you are successful, you may suddenly find that there are others aiming for your position, just as you yourself once aimed in that direction. There are those who may even want to be successful at your expense. Others may not want to harm you directly but will, nevertheless, want to know what you are doing so that they may emulate your success. And once these other individuals have reached *your* level of achievement, they may supply that little intangible "something" which will put them a step ahead of you.

When I first became a success as an acrobatic dancer, I was in the odd—and I must admit, enviable—position of having a unique act. Naturally, this gave me a tremendous advantage and I was able to command what was at that time an unheard-of salary. But no sooner did I achieve stardom than I started to watch out for hitherto unknown dancers who began to imitate my act. It wasn't that I was scared of imitations (for they are rarely as successful as the "originals" themselves are); it was just that I had to watch out for those who might come up with a possible feat or two that could make their act more popular than the one I had to offer.

I became extremely cautious about my "imitators", and instead of showing scorn for them, I concentrated on the areas of my own dance act which they might adopt for themselves and possibly improve upon. When I was in Paris, I received reports from as far off as South Africa, where these imitators were receiving recognition. I realized that once the entertainment world became flooded with acts similar to mine, the demand for my act would be lowered. If the competition really became fierce, I might even find myself without a job.

I had reached the point where I knew I had to do more than I was doing already. It wasn't sufficient merely to combine acrobatics with elegance in my performance—I had to master dance steps audiences had never seen before. If possible, I had to make sure these were dance steps only *I* could do that well. I also concentrated a great deal on increasing my publicity, for I could not afford to have my name less well-known than the names of other acrobatic dancers.

Just as I had in the dance field, I had to make sure exactly where my competition lay when I became successful in different areas of the business world. Once again, I had to recognize who the competitors were and what they could possibly do, directly or indirectly, to my career. I soon grew to realize that the dance field was hardly the only one in which fierce competition existed. And I also learned that the only way to cope with competition was to improve my product constantly.

When *Newsweek* was published for the first time, the

already successful *Time* developed extraordinary improvements in both style and content. When the perennially popular Ritz cracker began receiving competition from other firms, a "new, improved" Ritz cracker came out. And only a short while after the Kimberly-Clark Corporation began winning acceptance with Kleenex tissues, about a dozen other similar products were being offered to the public. Consequently, Kimberly-Clark improved its product even further, maintaining its lead in the field.

It matters little in what area you find yourself successful, if you're really *that* successful there will be imitators. Expect them to appear. Don't be upset when they show themselves, for they are actually a compliment to your own brand of originality and foresight. Learn how you can perfect what you are doing. Try to imagine what additional benefits you or your product have to offer.

Above all, keep up your research to improve yourself or your product in all areas where your position might be threatened. By remaining one step ahead of your potential competitors, your lasting success will be assured.

Your Image: Can You Hold On To It?

In our previous chapter on the achievement of the success goal, one of our rules concerned the concept of building an "image". To some extent, we have seen what this word means when it is applied to our particular success pattern.

Preserving this "image" is of equal importance in holding on to success. There are many images that never seem to change (the images of Rolls-Royce, Coca-Cola, and Cary Grant are excellent examples). It's not easy to build an image, and once that image appears before your public, every effort should be made to keep it the way it is. Otherwise, you may find yourself headed for a bit of trouble.

Of course, it would be absurd to tell yourself you must get involved in a scandal because it will help your image. What you must ask yourself is: "Because of my particular position in life, will such a risk hurt what I have achieved?" In our next chapter, we will explore the effects of such aspects of our civilization as sex and drinking on success itself. We will see, as we examine each of these factors, the effect they have on maintaining our image.

If by some unfortunate stroke of luck, we find, once we have achieved success, that our image is slipping—or possibly disappearing altogether—then and only then should we try to build a new one, rather than try to regain the image we've lost. Many prominent individuals have done exactly that and succeeded with equal brilliance a second, a third, and sometimes a fourth time.

But for the time being, while our present image is working successfully for us, we must make every effort to maintain it. Thus, our next and most important rule is:

Maintain the image with which you have made your success.

There is a rule that is very closely allied to the one about our image.

While you are constantly striving to maintain your particular image, you must also be aware of the constant changes in the world around you. The public's taste is often so unpredictable that it may begin a fad and drop it within a period of several months, or it may cling to the fad for a much longer period of time than you would have imagined possible.

What determines the public's taste may be the changing world itself. As one particular standard of morals disappears, a topless bathing suit makes headlines in the fashion world. When the threat of imminent disaster occurs in Asia, the stock market drops in New York.

In short, everything that happens in the world has an effect on everything else. If you want to remain a success, you must be aware of important changes, regardless of whether or not they pertain to your field. It's amazing, sometimes, how the most seemingly unrelated bit of information can be of use to you.

You must be most aware of the type of information which concerns what's going on in your particular field. To do this, you must read the important trade publications in your field. If you're involved in an aspect of the financial industry, it would be inconceivable for you to go without reading *Barron's* and *The Wall Street Journal*. If you are in show business, you would naturally read *Variety* every Wednesday afternoon. And if you work in the field of advertising, you will not miss a copy of *Advertising Age*.

But in addition to the trade journals, you should read at least one morning newspaper from front to back and, if possible, an evening paper, too. Watch news reports and panel discussions on TV; try to keep up with the latest trends in world affairs, books, art, and medicine. Directly or indirectly, some of the information you will come across is going to help you—or at least it will condition your business thinking along significant contemporary lines.

A very successful recent TV commercial parodies the James Bond type of melodrama. If the creative people involved in producing this commercial had not been familiar with a current trend in public taste, it is doubtful that they would have dreamed up such an effective piece of advertising.

I know of a young artist who has led a fairly secluded life, devoting nearly all of his time to his painting. His work has been exhibited in a number of small museums and galleries throughout Europe, but while travelling from one country to the other, the artist achieved only a small measure of success, painting in a style which art critics label "abstract expressionism". Being unhappy with his lack of success, he decided to bring himself up-to-date with the newest trends in painting.

One afternoon, while living in Brussels, the artist came across a series of articles in *Life* magazine on so-called "pop-art". The articles intrigued him so much, he flew back to this country and has since devoted himself almost exclusively to working in the "pop art" field, one he had, up until that time, known nothing about. Within a very short time, the artist not only achieved considerable recognition—not to mention financial remuneration—but he also found this art form far more exciting to work with than any previous style he had used. Had he scoffed at the idea of keeping up with current trends, this young man would still be struggling merely to keep himself alive.

There is an almost interminable list of cases of successful people and firms that ultimately failed simply because they did not take advantage of the changes going on around them. Companies that manufactured buttons could easily have gone into the zipper business when the zipper came out on the market had they only recognized the importance of the new invention.

There is one particular case involving a large oil company which was situated in a South American country but was owned and operated by North Americans. Almost overnight, an influential political group sprang up in the South American country and began making capital out of the fact that North Americans had controlling interest in their oil. This political group insisted that the interests be given back to their fellow countrymen. The indications were indeed ominous—at least for the firm in the United States, which should have taken heed of the fact that the political group was gaining more and more headway and before long would probably control the entire country.

Instead of doing the logical thing—selling their interests at once—the executives of the American firm entirely disregarded the threats and, with undue optimism, decided to remain in the country and continue their operation of the oil company. Predictably, when the new government achieved control, the North American executives were forced out and had to sell their holdings at a depressing loss.

Members of the British steel industry have learned to pay strict attention to political developments in their own country. Before the Labour Party came into power in England, they knew quite well that the entire industry would be affected.

Members of the watch-making industry pay close attention to what happens in the electronic world, for if enough watches are put on the market with electronic devices, it is imperative that these watch firms take advantage of this development.

The information you absorb should have the largest scope possible. You must know about taxes and what makes them rise and fall. You should have a strong comprehension of the problems in the world today so that you can foresee any threats to your industry.

During my dancing career in the United States, I was constantly aware of trends in the entertainment industry. But I also had equal knowledge of important events in the country as a whole. When I learned that the United States government was clamping down on charge accounts in night clubs, I sensed at once that the night-club business in this country would fall off considerably and that I might have difficulty securing a top job or commanding the salary I had been accustomed to receiving. I therefore prepared at once for a European tour, putting myself way ahead of other dancers when they discovered, too late, that their jobs in the United States were being threatened.

It's all part of the same rule:

Be aware of the changing world.

Once you become successful, it is inevitable that you will serve as a kind of reverse mirror to the unsuccessful person. He recognizes your success and becomes infinitely more aware of his own lack of it. In fact, as a success you become a symbol of what the unsuccessful person cannot be. Regardless of how objective he may be, he is destined to experience envy and may tend to minimize your success or even negate it entirely.

The result often takes the form of unmitigated hostility directed towards the successful person.

Every political leader has experienced an extreme form of this type of reaction. But it was Harry S. Truman who came up with the best answer: "If you can't stand the heat, get out of the kitchen." And that's pretty much my advice to you.

I have never known a truly successful person who hasn't had at least one of the following things happen to him: he has lost one or more close friends; he has been openly and brutally attacked in the newspapers and/or radio and TV; he has received a chain of nasty anonymous letters; he has become the subject of an unwarranted and upsetting lawsuit; his marriage has gone on the rocks; he has been blackmailed.

Now, after glancing over the above list of rather horrendous happenings, you may consider you would be far better off being *unsuccessful*. What you must realize, however, is that being successful sometimes creates a disturbing alchemy among individuals and their particular relationships. But if you are made of the stuff which makes successful people *remain* that way, it will have little or no importance if one of the above things should happen to you.

Every political leader knows he will be attacked during the course of his career. Winston Churchill was spat upon in the streets. Lincoln was one of the most reviled men of his age.

Remember this important fact:

To remain successful, the best thing for you to do is prepare yourself for conflict and hostility.

After a while you will learn how to cope with the kind of attacks that occur when you are successful. You will begin to see these attacks for what they really are: merely the outlet unsuccessful people use to cover up their own frustration at not being in your position. Strangely enough, if these unsuccessful individuals should reach the same positon as you, they would begin to see you in an entirely different light.

If you find you are operating in an area where, let's say, you're thrust into the public eye, then the sort of attack I mention will occur quite frequently. But you might try an interesting experiment if the attack upsets you: simply go to the library and read through editorials in back copies of newspapers written ten, twenty, or possibly fifty years ago. You will come across several pieces of writing that will undoubtedly amuse you. You may read about a now famous industrialist whose offbeat business methods were brutally criticized when they were first introduced to his firm. In newspapers published before World War II, you will find colums attacking world leaders who wanted to stop Hitler at any cost. And when you read over the book reviews, you will be amazed at how many Pulitzer Prize novelists were advised to give up their craft by certain critics.

Making Success Permanent

The worst thing a successful person can do is to try to mitigate the attack by yielding to it—in a sense, to "reform". At all costs, you must try to avoid the unhappy business of trying to please the world, for you have to consider that it was your own foresight and unique method of handling a situation that placed you in your present position.

There is the case of a very prominent newspaperman who is probably the most despised individual in his entire profession. He has been the subject of numerous and quite vicious attacks for his uncompromising frankness, and once at a party (I know this is true because I saw it happen), a fairly well-known politician tossed a drink in this man's face.

The following morning, the journalist was back at his typewriter, turning out a column in the usual manner. Not one ounce of toughness had been leavened. His articles were as frank and as hostility-provoking as ever. The reason: this man knows quite well what his readers want, and the moment he wavers, he will lose every last one of them.

Our next rule then is:

Don't be a victim of sensitivity.

Remember that the moment people stop envying you the chances are you are losing your foothold on success.

One March evening in 1956, when I was performing in a night club in Melbourne, Australia, a robust-looking gentleman came backstage to tell the entire cast how much he enjoyed the show. The warmth and enormous graciousness of this stranger, together with what came across as an unusual combination of politeness and self-assurance, told me at once that this was a man who was truly successful in his particular field. Afterwards, I learned from the other members of the cast that he was the great Oscar Hammerstein II.

Looking back on the meeting with Hammerstein now, I recall with pleasure his extraordinary personality. When a member of the cast joked with him or asked him a question, he responded as naturally and as guilelessly as if we were all his closest friends. There wasn't an ounce of self-conscious superiority in his personality. He was simply someone who had liked our show and wanted to tell us about it. His mere behaviour was an advertisement of his success.

I remember contrasting this meeting with Hammerstein to a meeting I had several years later with the head of a real-estate company whom others had described as being "a recent success". The real-estate man was trying to interest a group of us in investments in some property. In recent months, he had carried out a number of promising business ventures, and our group was indeed quite anxious—at least in the beginning—to be involved in future building projects organized by him.

After being with the man for no more than ten minutes, however, I realized that he was not long destined to be a success. For one thing, he was so obviously intoxicated with his own recent rise in the industry that it seemed as if it were *he* who was doing *us* the favour, rather than the other way around. Not only did he display little disturbing personality traits—like not looking directly at us when he spoke—but he told us bluntly that if we didn't go along with his ideas he could quite easily toss us aside and interest another group. Meanwhile, he emphasized very few of the benefits we might reap as a result of our investment.

Our group emerged from this somewhat peculiar business meeting more than a little baffled. None of us could understand why the man was behaving in such a strange manner. Though it was true some of his business dealings in the past had made him quite successful, he was hardly in the position to treat prospective associates in such a coldly disdainful manner.

Of course, after that, we had little interest in joining him in his real-estate projects, and it was about a year later that we learned that he had gone bankrupt. I am convinced that his utterly supercilious manner was what eventually ruined him.

One of the great tragedies of achieving success is the negative effect such an achievement seems to have on certain people. For a psychological reason I have never been able to comprehend, these people feel the moment they've achieved what they want they are almost required by the laws of nature to behave in a superior manner toward others. It's as if they are suddenly omnipotent—absolutely nothing bad can touch them now that the gods have bestowed on them such lavish gifts.

But this unfortunate frame of mind could very well destroy them entirely. They tend to overplay their hands; they throw caution to the winds; they antagonize the very people whom they should cultivate; and their feelings of self-importance become so exaggerated in their minds that they fail to see their own limitations.

I'm not saying that there's anything wrong with elation over your achievements. But you must continue to maintain a hold on reality or else you're unquestionably destined for failure.

If you are truly a successful individual, you must understand that others will recognize this fact without your trying to exaggerate it. But once you start displaying an over-impressive kind of façade, others will become suspicious. They will tend to doubt that you are really as successful as you claim to be and see the façade for what it really is: *insecurity*.

At the present time, I know two men, both of whom happen to be in the field of advertising and both of whom have scored an almost equal measure of success. I feel I can predict now which one of them will probably go on to perform even greater things and which will probably destroy his success entirely.

The latter is head of a large advertising agency. In recent months, I have noticed that he has been spending more and more time trying desperately to build up the prestige of his name by attending an inordinate number of social functions. I wonder, in fact, how he has time to take care of his own business. Also, he has an excellent press agent who makes certain he is mentioned more and more frequently in society columns. In short, he seems far more involved in making others know *his* name rather than what is obviously the sole purpose of his business—letting them know *the names of his clients*.

Now there is nothing wrong with publicity for the successful man. In fact, it is essential. But when, as in this case, that publicity centres entirely on the man's meaningless social identification, it becomes ultimately useless publicity.

In addition to the emphasis on himself in the newspapers, this man has also grown practically intolerable in his relationships with people. I understand he has even begun to ignore his staff unless he is issuing a particular order, and he will almost never bother to converse with people he considers in a lower echelon of the advertising industry.

The case of the second person is entirely different. If anything, his success seems to have made him so secure that his good nature is extended to everyone, particularly the people who work for him and who, he realizes, have undoubtedly contributed to his success. Whenever you have conversations with this second advertising man, you are amazed at how he always remembers to discuss your personal interests and problems. And never for one moment is he patronizing or aloof.

I have watched truly successful and brilliant businessmen at board meetings, and I am always a little surprised at how restrained they are. They will say very little unless they have to—and above all, they never want to dominate the discussion merely to hear the sound of their own voices. If the situation calls for it, they will never fail to smile or inject a note of humour into what they have to say, and they will make sure they let others who have differing opinions and points of view express these opinions.

I am always suspicious of the somewhat jumpy individual who makes sure to seat himself near the head of the board table and is constantly shouting out his views and shouting down everybody else's. This man, it is quite obvious, wants to overcompensate for some lack. Everyone else will recognize his insecurity, and it will hardly provide anyone with faith in his business ideas.

I am reminded here of a business conference I once witnessed between two enormously successful corporation heads, who were meeting for the first time. Each, obviously, had a battle to fight and had come to fight it, for the two corporations were joining hands in a dual investment, and each corporation chairman apparently had a different idea about how that investment was to be made.

Almost at once, the chairman in whose office the meeting was held turned on the other with a show of force I have rarely witnessed in the business world. He brutally tore apart the other man's ideas, pointing out the lack of feasibility of the other's plans concerning the investment, and not once did he permit the other chairman to interject a comment until he had finished saying his piece.

The entire time, the other company head sat, taking in every word with a faint smile on his lips. I couldn't help studying this curious picture, for here was a top man in his industry, worth several million dollars in his own right, sitting quietly by while another man (and one less powerful than he) shouted him down.

Finally, the vociferous chairman stopped speaking. He stared a moment at the other company head without saying a word; it was obvious that he, too, was puzzled by the latter's calm exterior. Everyone in the room seemed to fear an explosion at that point.

Instead, the company head upon whom the attack had been made faced the attacker squarely and, still smiling, asked placidly, "Have you finished?"

The anxiety-ridden chairman nodded and took his seat at his desk while the other chairman stunned us all by shrugging his shoulders and saying, "Well, I won't argue with you when you're right. And frankly your argument appears to be right—but I don't understand what all the shouting was about."

The perturbed executive turned red. He couldn't quite believe what was happening. In a matter of seconds, the other man had quite agreeably gone along with his plans!

The troubled man quickly apologized for having behaved so rudely. He offered as his defence what was obviously true: he had heard so much about the powerful corporation head that he was literally terrified of him, so terrified that he was certain the other would never agree to his plans unless he was, in a sense, bullied into carrying them out.

Both men became most gracious at that point and laughed good-naturedly. The outburst was quickly forgotten, and we all went to work discussing the business at hand.

The incident struck me as interesting from several standpoints. First of all, it revealed to me once again that powerful people in the business world sometimes have glaring weaknesses. In the case of one man, his weakness had simply been his misdirected plans for the mutual investment. In the case of the second person, the weakness took an emotional form in his irrational outburst.

But more important, the incident showed that here were two men—both of whom were at the top of their particular field—who were far above the petty hostilities that grip a great many people. The attacked corporation head could quite readily have met anger with anger, and there would have ensued a pointless, painful quarrel that probably would have had disastrous results. Instead, he remained quietly listening to the other's ideas and even agreed to them once he saw they were right. The angry corporation head, meanwhile, emphasized his own identity as a success by graciously apologizing for his unwarranted outburst. And when both men quickly got down to the business of the day, almost oblivious to the fact that any emotional display had taken place between them, I knew that these were truly successful individuals, who were able to differentiate between what was really important in their lives and what was not.

I have noticed a similar parallel among university instructors. It is always the *very secure, very successful* professor who will listen to everything his students have to say, regardless of how inane or insignificant a particular question appears to others. The rather weak instructor, troubled by his own standing and prestige, is generally the one who subtly or not so subtly belittles a student.

Polite self-assurance remains the dominant trait in the truly successful man.

I am reminded of an incident involving the late Albert Einstein. This genius and marvellously humane man was attending a luncheon given in his honour at New York's Waldorf-Astoria. At the door, not recognizing who he was, the head-waiter told Einstein he couldn't enter the large room where the luncheon was being held, for Einstein was dressed in a very casual manner, tieless and wearing a sports jacket and sweater.

When he was asked to leave, Einstein very calmly turned from the doorway. He was on his way home to change into more appropriate garb for the occasion before an eagle-eyed guest spotted the scientist and managed to stop him at the lift.

Einstein could have been terribly affronted. He could have ranted at great length about the apparent mistreatment he had received from the head-waiter. But this marvellous man had enough sense to know it would probably have cost him too much in emotional energy—energy he could much more beneficially direct towards his work. The way he behaved was a testimony not only to his inner security but to his extra-ordinary success.

It's important, when you're successful, not to fight for small causes, not to dissipate your energies in unimportant directions which have nothing whatever to do with main-taining your success. There's no point at all in trying to prove your superiority to a nameless group of individuals who, in actuality, mean nothing to your life and care little about your future.

Always consider exactly how relevant your emotional re-actions are; show your self-assurance but remain gracious— all of which goes under the heading of our next rule:

Wear success well.

We might, at this point, consider what is a sort of subsid-iary rule to the above. And that is:

Respect the success of others.

Making Success Permanent

A prominent architect, a friend of mine, once told me a story about himself and an equally prominent member of his field. Both men ran firms which seemed to attract similar groups of clients, and curiously enough they continued to remain good friends, showing little or no animosity or jealousy regarding each other's success.

One afternoon, the architect with whom I am friendly received a surprise telephone call from an organization which was currently setting up plans to build a community centre. Though the organization had originally planned to employ the rival architect to carry out the project, my friend's plans were so excellent that, at the last minute, the executives of the organization had changed their minds and were handing the project over to him.

Now at the same time that my friend was delighted with the decision, he knew quite well how upset the other architect would be. To make matters even more awkward, the two men had agreed to play golf the following Saturday afternoon. My friend was tempted to cancel the appointment, convinced that there would be nothing but hard feelings on the part of his business rival. Nevertheless, after giving the matter much thought, he decided to go through with the golf match.

It was no small measure of surprise that awaited my friend the following Saturday. His business rival greeted him as jovially as usual, without the slightest betrayal of anger or jealousy, and the two men played their game of golf without a single mention of what obviously must have represented an enormous "slap in the face" to one and a victory to the other.

At the end of the game, which my friend lost by a small margin, the other architect slung one arm about my friend's shoulder and said, "Well, Ed, I guess you can't win 'em all".

That was the first and only time that my friend's business rival made a reference to the lost account. My friend returned home that evening, filled with admiration for the other architect's magnificent display of good will in a matter which undoubtedly must have cost him quite a bit of disappointment.

One of the chief characteristics of a truly successful person is his ability to withstand setbacks and to treat with admiration—not envy—those who are also successful. By showing others that you respect their success, you actually show that you belong to their class, that you understand how difficult it is to achieve what they have achieved.

Have you ever watched two opposing Counsels at a trial? The pair may rant and rave at one another during the course of the courtroom proceedings, but during recess you might very easily find them having lunch at the same table in a restaurant near the court.

It is good practice to admire sincerely others' successes. By doing so, you indirectly associate yourself with their good fortune. But by remaining in a frustrated, jealous frame of mind you are removing yourself from the "atmosphere" of success. Chances are if you keep behaving in that manner, your own insecurity will get the better of you. Others will learn to regard your sour disposition as a sure sign of failure, and within a short period of time, you will actually become one.

Remember: one of the sure ways to hold on to success is to cultivate successful people, not only in your own field but in all areas of life. If you respect their accomplishments, they will undoubtedly respect yours. And in time they will help you achieve even more than your present success has brought you.

Making Success Permanent

Here, now, is our list of rules for holding on to the success we already have:

1. Keep up your drive.
2. Follow new directions.
3. Watch out for competition which may threaten your success.
4. Maintain the image with which you have made your success.
5. Be aware of the changing world.
6. Don't be a victim of sensitivity.
7. Wear success well.
8. Respect the success of others.

We have covered in some detail the way we should behave in order to achieve success—and we have just examined a set of rules which we should follow once that success becomes ours. Now, however, we are at a point in our book where we want to take a look at what happens to some of us in our *personal lives* once we become successful and how these happenings affect our success.

Some of the points will seem a little astonishing. I don't, for example, believe it's impossible for an alcoholic to be an enormously successful individual. I am also firmly convinced that, in certain cases, a man may lead the most recklessly immoral life and maintain every bit of his success.

Exactly what these specific cases are, and how important it is for us to recognize whether they would apply to us, are among the matters I should like now to discuss.

6 Success as a Way of Life

I HAVE ALWAYS BEEN A LITTLE AMAZED—AND MORE OFTEN than not, intrigued—when I renew a friendship with a person who, at one time, I knew to be unsuccessful but who is now at the top of his particular profession or field. What strikes my interest more than anything else perhaps is this individual's attitude towards aspects of life which before he seemed to take for granted.

Money is one of these aspects. I have seen, in some rather unfortunate cases, people who regarded money in a relaxed comfortable manner throughout their struggle for success, but the moment they "made it", their attitude completely changed.

Sex—or perhaps I should say your attitude towards sex— is still another aspect. In some cases, your point of view about marriage changes. And so, occasionally, does your attitude towards the law and ethics.

136

Success as a Way of Life

No matter how "special" the individual considers himself, once he has achieved his success goal, he must realize that somehow or other conflicts will arise between his success and the world around him. Exactly how he should behave in regard to these possible conflicts is one of the matters I plan to discuss in this chapter.

While reading this chapter and applying the principles discussed here to your own success, there is one important point to keep constantly in mind:

In this book we are concerned with one thing and one thing only—the *achievement* and *maintenance* of success. Anything not relative to this, whether it involves, let's say, religious beliefs or, possibly, a question of moral judgement, does not interest us here. The only point that we are considering in this chapter particularly is whether what we do has a good or adverse effect on the maintenance of our success.

Now let us examine the categories themselves and their various relationships to our success.

Success and Money

There are two separate points I hope to make here, and I hope they do not appear to contradict one another. The first concerns *indifference* to money, while the second concerns the time when money should receive our undivided attention.

Let's take the first point.

Someone once came to me in the hope that I would organize a financial group to invest in a project which would eliminate the need for carbon paper by office-workers. At least on a superficial level, the project excited me a great deal, and I was eager to put my time and effort into the matter. Later, when I mentioned to a friend that I was busily organizing this financial group, telling him how involved I was in the project and how much confidence I had in it, the first question my friend asked me was: "How much money will you make?"

Frankly, I was appalled.

I tried, rather futilely, I suppose, to explain to my friend a premise I've always believed to be true: that a truly successful person must think of the project first, for if the project is well conceived it automatically involves financial remuneration. Making money, *per se*, I stressed, is only a valid premise if money *itself* is your major aim.

I have always found this premise to be correct. It simply *has to be*, for it is only natural in this society that success is translated into terms of money—a factor which holds true in any business and in any profession, regardless of whether the individual is the owner of a major textile firm or is a prominent surgeon.

It was impossible to convey this idea to my friend. It was at that point that I realized there was something entirely negative in his business thinking, that he thought only in terms of money without defining it as a major aim. As a result, I knew, he was destined to be a fairly confused and therefore unsuccessful man. For one thing, he simply did not understand what money really was.

What happens in the thinking of this type of person is that he gives money itself primary consideration, as opposed to the *major aim*, which in my case was obviously to get the office project on the market.

Nearly all my life I've thought in terms of success first and let the money fall in its more natural, secondary position, knowing of course it would come to me in time. My primary interest has always been to create the product. Then, once every aspect of the product is polished, *I will price that product very high*. But you cannot possibly do this if you're going to worry about the immediate dollar. If you do, you lose sight of the bigger goal and wind up, if you're lucky, with one *little goal.* And in achieving little goals you can hardly be considered successful.

In my dancing career, while I was making a decent salary, many people asked me why I hadn't taken other jobs to supplement my income. *Why?* Because I was busy during that extra time, polishing the dance act I had already developed so that it would be perfected to the utmost degree. Before long, my investment of time paid off. And when one considers my over-all earnings covering a period of several years they are, naturally enough, far greater than they would have been if I had devoted that extra time and effort to other jobs.

In a sense, it's the same sort of thing in the business world. Let's suppose, for example, you're an enormously successful manufacturer of a particular kind of electronic device which has a wide market that you are yet unable to supply. It would be foolish for you to look for other markets until you satisfied the present one.

By the same token, it would be ridiculous for you as an executive of a big firm to pause and figure out what your stocks are worth every day. The sensible thing to do would be to leave them alone and concentrate on the work of improving the corporation itself. Executives do not tremble over the momentary value of their stocks on the market. If they did, they would be in a state of continuous, unbearable anxiety and would hardly be capable of running their business.

On the other hand, if you develop an attitude of irreverence towards money, concentrating more on the success of the particular enterprise you are creating, your chances for achieving monetary success also are far greater.

Let money be a by-product. Consider the project in terms

of its bigness. By craving for success, rather than money alone, the money will inevitably come.

Now from irreverence towards money we pass to our second point—which concerns those moments when more than a certain amount of reverence is necessary.

Success and Financial Planning

One afternoon, not too long ago, I had an experience which jolted me.

I happened to pick up a copy of a daily newspaper and came across a recent photograph of a once prominent member of the sports world, a former welter-weight champion boxer and, incidentally, one of my personal idols. I could not believe the photograph or the caption, but there it was—a sad and familiar story, presented as graphically as possible.

The former boxer, who during the course of his short but active career had earned more than a million dollars, was shown standing outside a run-down shack in a Southern backwater town. He and his children had just built a soft-drink stand to help them make enough money to live on, and they were shown holding drinks out to some customers.

What happened to this sports figure's phenomenal earnings?

Well, when you think about a possible answer to this question, you'll realize there's no special trick to ridding yourself of your money. However, as much as my sympathy goes out to this once famous member of the sports world, I also feel that there's no excuse for letting all that money disappear in so short a time.

How often have you picked up a newspaper and read the case of a famous film star who has died virtually penniless? The majority of theatre people and athletes have comparatively short careers and must learn to invest some of their earnings if they hope, in later years, to have any sort of income. But film stars and athletes aren't the only ones who have to cope with this problem.

Let's suppose your particular success involves making a great deal of money. The next thing you're going to have to do is protect that money so that you won't lose what you've made.

I've observed the, to me, incredible situation that arises when an extraordinarily successful man hands over some of his earnings to an unsuccessful man to invest for him. A prominent textile manufacturer I know recently handed the profits he earned in a clever business manoeuvre to a second-rate brokerage house. It might have taken an hour's research to find out the exact standing of this brokerage house. Instead, the manufacturer's hasty action cost him a fortune.

I think investments are a wise and important consideration for every successful man. But they should be made very cautiously.

I myself allocate a comparatively small amount of money each year with which I take calculated business gambles. Proceeding in this manner, nothing too drastic can possibly happen to me no matter how badly the investments turn out.

The important thing to do, if you want to maintain your financial security and at the same time enjoy the variety of pleasures that come from investing in uncertain business ventures, is to invest only a small percentage of your income —a percentage which you know won't ruin you financially if you happen to lose it.

Let's suppose I take seven of these so-called calculated risks within the next four years. I'm still ahead of the game if, in the fourth year, one of these ventures happens to pay off. And once that seventh investment pays off, I must consider that I can't afford to invest all the money I make with it in an eighth uncertain enterprise. Once again, I must invest merely a small portion of these unanticipated business earnings.

By following this simple pattern, which I enjoy calling the "seven-year calculated business risk" method, you can keep your investments going, you can have fun with them, and chances are you will ultimately establish financial security for yourself. In a sense, what you are doing is exactly what you did in the past to provide your success: you are increasing your mathematical odds for your financial security.

Success and Sex

One morning, I had to take part in an important business meeting, the first in a series of meetings involving a joint project sponsored by four separate companies. I was representing one of the companies.

Each of the four representatives had these things in common: we were all very successful in our respective fields, and we were bachelors.

Our meeting was scheduled for 10.00 A.M. at the board room of one of the companies. Three of us arrived promptly at the scheduled time, but it wasn't until 10.45 that the fourth member of our group showed up. I had met this individual a number of times in the past, and he had always struck me as an extremely nice, amusing young man who had done remarkably well for himself in the business world, considering his age and comparative lack of experience. The young man had also displayed to me an extraordinarily shrewd business sense, and therefore I was quite surprised that he had arrived so late at so important a meeting—a meeting in which some highly significant business plans of his particular company were to be discussed. As surprised as I was by his late arrival, I was flabbergasted by what happened shortly thereafter.

A moment or so after he sat down at the board table, the young man embarked on a lengthy explanation as to why he was so late, proceeding to tell us a rather descriptive story of how he had met a voluptuous and sexy young lady the evening before. He had spent the entire night with her in bed, he admitted with a twinkle in his eye. He then went on to tell us that because she was so marvellous a love partner, he couldn't bear the thought of sending her home early in the morning. The young man was sure, since each of us was a bachelor, we would understand.

As the young man finished relating his story, which he undoubtedly expected would win our complete sympathies, I glanced at the faces of the other two company representatives. It was as if an electric current had just sent a shock through the room. They sat there stupefied. Finally, one of the men laughed embarrassedly, while the other merely remarked coldly, "Don't you think it's time we got down to some business?"

Naturally, this young man had made a blunder. But it was also more than that. I could tell, right then and there, his attitude was a foreshadowing of his eventual downfall in the business world.

The months passed. As it turned out, the joint project of the four companies fell through, and so I lost touch with the young man for a while. In view of the failure of the project—which was not the fault of any of the four representatives—one might consider that the young man's *faux pas* at the business meeting hardly mattered. But the idea remained with me that the way the young man had behaved was important simply because it was *indicative* of other things he did. He was making one of the most serious mistakes any really successful person can make: he was mixing sex with business.

Then, one afternoon, I ran into the young man on the street. He greeted me as amiably as ever, but he was distinctly troubled. He told me that he was now working for another, less prominent, company. He missed his old job, he remarked sadly, and he wasn't doing especially well in his current position. In a sense, he felt it might be the beginning of the end for him, and I suspected that he might be right.

Looking back on the incident of the business meeting, I realize the young man made two mistakes: the first was letting the romp with his sensuous girl friend interfere with the business meeting; and the second was telling us about it. It would have been far more delicate to state simply that he had been detained for personal reasons and let it go at that. Had the young man described his amorous adventure over five-o'clock cocktails, the three of us would have enjoyed it. But his story, told at an important meeting, only pointed to the young man's frivolous disregard of his business obligations.

I have seen incidents of this type occur with many, many businessmen, and it never fails to amaze me that people who are so mature in every other aspect of their business dealings can be so lighthearted when it comes to incorporating sex into the work-a-day world. Sex simply has no place in the business or professional life of the successful individual.

Still another example of the sort of thing I mean occurred recently when a highly successful advertising executive— a man I had met only briefly through some mutual business acquaintances—began establishing a reputation for himself as "the fellow no model is safe in the same office with". The executive had a job in which he spent a good part of his day interviewing beautiful young women for advertising spots in magazines and on TV. Before long, obviously, the job had gone to his head. As the stories went, no sooner would a beautiful young woman step into his office for an interview than a pair of hands would fly about her waist, and this office Casanova would begin re-enacting a scene he had just witnessed in the latest Doris Day-Rock Hudson film. Soon, the other executives at his agency were in an uproar, not so much because he was making a play for the models who visited the office (that was bad enough), but because all the really worthwhile models were refusing to work for the agency. Before long, only the second-rate models—the ones who felt they had to put up with this man's shenanigans to get work—were arriving for interviews.

Consequently, the agency itself began losing clients and soon the amorous executive was out of a job.

Now all of this has nothing to do with the moral question involved. Frankly, from our standpoint—that of *holding on* to success—if you can keep your sex life reasonably discreet and apart from your profession or business dealings, it doesn't matter whether you lead what might be considered the most "debauched" or "amoral" personal life. The point is that sex should *remain* a personal side of life and never, for one moment, show its head through the door of an office.

Contrary to an all-too-common misconception, on a level of real, solid business success, sex never interferes. The highly successful stage director or "glamour" photographer who spends a good portion of his time interviewing some of the most radiantly beautiful women around town will almost never become involved with the girls he sees professionally. And in the instances where he does, he will not permit these involvements to interfere with the work itself.

The same holds true for the myth about "the boss and his secretary who really understands him". I have rarely witnessed this kind of relationship among truly successful individuals. A man may be the head of a large corporation and have four separate mistresses set up in apartments at various places throughout the city, but he will avoid embarking on an affair with his Gal Friday, simply because in doing so he knows he is risking his success and everything to which he has devoted a major share of his life.

I'm not denying for one moment that the boss-secretary after-hours relationship is a prevalent phenomenon of the business world. But it exists almost entirely on a lower-echelon level. And I know the moment I hear of this kind of relationship that the businessman in question is someone not destined to be very successful, for whether he realizes it or not, success is not really his *primary* goal in life.

I don't believe I or anyone else should sit in judgment of an individual for his particular sex habits, however unique they may appear to the average person. Let that person become involved in whatever sexual escapades he chooses. And some of the most successful people in the world have the wildest, most uninhibited sex lives anyone might imagine. But the reason these individuals remain successful is that they keep sex as something that functions only "after hours".

I know another case of a remarkably handsome, wealthy, and only recently married Park Avenue physician who, over the past ten years, has numbered among his patients some of the most beautiful show girls and models in New York. I know as a fact that a number of these women—possibly because they considered it a challenge—have made sexual overtures to this young doctor. And I know also that he has pleasantly and tactfully rejected every one of these overtures.

His reason for having done so is obvious. One indiscretion could very easily wreck everything he has built up in his practice.

It boils down, simply, to what we've been saying all along. Sex—like everything else—is fine to any degree or in any form you may wish providing it doesn't interfere with maintaining your success.

Someone else will have to write a book on whether it is "immoral" or "ethical", let's say, to have a wife and children and still keep one or more mistresses on the side. That's not my concern. I say, keep as many as you like—providing they never see the inside of your office.

Success and Marriage

Just as in the categories already discussed, if you are a truly successful individual, marriage—if it enters your life—cannot be separated from your success.

On the surface, this statement may appear somewhat un-romantic. But think about it a moment. I certainly don't wish to imply that you should choose a wife simply because you make an attractive picture together at parties for fellow executives. On the contrary, marriage without love—or marriage based solely on "practical" grounds—can only hamper a man's success because of the frustrating lack of fulfilment an unsuccessful marriage provides. Also, a wife you love offers an emotional support that is invaluable.

But sometimes marriage must be streamlined to success. And I have seen successful persons do exactly that.

I am thinking now of two contrasting cases, both involving men who happen to love their wives and both of whom were fully aware of their wives' inadequacies. In the first instance, the marriage contributed to wrecking the husband's career.

In the second, the type of marriage the man has made seems to matter little.

I remember attending a party once given by a top-echelon executive of one corporation for top-echelon executives of a group of corporations, all more or less involved in the same industry. The couple in the first—the negative—example arrived late, and they made a sorry sight indeed. The moment they entered the room, all eyes fell upon them, and there was a long embarrassed hush over the gathering. The husband—incidentally, at that time one of the top men in his field—stood at the door nervously, nodding his greetings left and right and appearing so ill at ease it was almost impossible for anyone to communicate with him. The reason for his anxiety was all too apparent, for there, standing next to him, stood his wife, a large, overdressed woman who wore too much make-up and greeted everyone in a loud, overpowering manner.

As the evening wore on, the woman became more and more of an irritant, not only to the other guests at the gathering but mostly to her husband, whose own lack of poise reached such extremes that I found it almost impossible to believe the man was successful. Just as it seemed as if the husband were about to collapse entirely, he made his excuses, and tugging at his wife's elbow he led her quickly away from the gathering, much to everyone's relief.

Obviously, a number of the guests at the party had witnessed this type of scene before. Had the guests been a group from the couple's local community centre their reaction wouldn't have mattered that much. But these were people who *demanded*—and rightly so—that a top member of their industry behave in a more dignified manner.

The experience was unsettling, to say the least.

Months later, I learned that the hapless husband had "left"

his company. The last I heard of him, he and his wife were moving to a small town in the Middle West where the husband had been promised another, less impressive position.

Now I don't know whether this man's wife had any direct influence on her husband's ultimate failure. But I am convinced she must have contributed to it greatly. From every indication, the man functioned quite well in the business world, but when it came to attending a simple social function his prestige was virtually wrecked by the presence of a boorish wife.

In the second case, the wife was not so bad as the woman I've just described. But with a different attitude on the part of her husband, there might have been a similar outcome.

I met this couple at a party also, only this was a dinner party given for a large group of faculty members of a prominent university. The husband was a leader in his field. He had written several scholarly books, considered by many the best of their kind, and he had been asked to address the gathering after supper had been served.

In this case, the wife wasn't loud or overdressed. She was merely *silly*. Before dinner, this unfortunate woman continually interrupted other people's conversations with fatuous comments and even went so far as to tell a number of completely inappropriate, *risqué* jokes which were merely met with a few polite grins on the part of the other faculty members and their wives.

During the course of the evening, I kept observing the husband's reaction. It was truly amazing, for this eminent college professor stood at his wife's side, comfortably smiling and saying very little. It was obvious that he was used to his wife's behaviour, completely aware of the fact that nothing he could say or do would change her. He also must have realized that, by reacting negatively to her, he would only make matters worse.

It was clear to me that none of the other guests really liked the wife. But that didn't matter. *They still liked the professor himself* and respected him. It was almost as if the other faculty members were saying to themselves, "Well, if he loves her, that's his business. The main thing is that he is a supremely competent member of the academic field, respected by everyone. Why, even now, look how dignified he appears!"

I was convinced the professor's calm was about to be shattered, however, when he began making his after-dinner speech. Sitting at his left was his wife, who had obviously drunk a little too much and was emitting a series of audible giggles at various intervals during the professor's remarks. A number of times, the husband actually had to stop speaking because of his wife's incongruous laughter that interrupted what he had to say.

Finally, and still maintaining the utmost dignity, the college professor turned to face his wife and smiling graciously remarked with impeccable dignity, "Darling, I know I asked you to laugh appreciatively at what I had to say. But I do wish you would wait until I reach the *funny* part."

Naturally, everyone at the dinner was amused. We were utterly disarmed by this man's complete control of the situation. Even the wife seemed to understand at this point, and her nonsensical giggling ceased. The professor was telling us, in a sense, "Don't you see, my friends, the way my wife is behaving is very unimportant. She's merely displaying a few lovable idiosyncrasies."

I'm sure the other guests reacted as I did. We all "accepted" the wife now, and we respected the husband more than ever.

Success as a Way of Life

In the cases of most successful men I've seen, the wives complement the husbands to the point where they blend right into their husbands' success, helping them to maintain their images. In our century, the wives of Winston Churchill and Franklin Delano Roosevelt are two of the most outstanding examples of women who have been of invaluable help to their husbands in building their careers and, most important, helping their husbands once their success has been attained.

If by some stroke of fate, however, the successful man finds himself burdened with a wife who inspires a few shudders at social gatherings, the best thing he can do is treat her behaviour in a relaxed manner. After all, consider the primary fact: business associates are not really interested in the way your wife behaves, they're interested in you. By calling attention to your wife's inadequacies, you yourself come off as inadequate. But by remaining self-confident and poised at all times, you are inspiring trust.

In fact, an imaginative business contact might spot the way you are behaving and say to himself something on the order of: "Well, if he can cope with her, I'm sure he can cope with any problem."

Success and Advice from Business Acquaintances and Friends

An upstate New York corporation once approached me with an idea to organize an American branch of a European glass-manufacturing company. At the time, the company was chiefly concerned with the development of a new technique for building houses, utilizing a material known as "glass brick". The concept of building an entire house along the same lines as one made of brick, with one block of glass cemented to another, intrigued me a great deal, and I began considering the corporation's offer very seriously.

Since this type of business was entirely new to me, I decided to find out the reactions of some of the people I knew who were in the glass industry, the building industry, and the general area of finance.

A curious thing occurred.

Of the fifteen friends and business acquaintances I approached, I received fifteen completely varying opinions, ranging from "horrible" to "stupendous".

At first, I didn't know what to make of these opinions. My bafflement lasted for several days. I must admit I was more confused than ever as to whether I should embark on this particular project. Then, finally, I decided to investigate matters further, to see if I could uncover any reason for the extraordinarily divergent viewpoints.

I soon learned some interesting things. The people I had questioned were judging the project not as it related to *me* but as it related to *them*. I discovered, for instance, that one of my friends, a member of the glass industry, had downgraded the project, because, very simply, he didn't want me in the glass industry. How did I know? When I began to suspect that he felt this way and asked him about it, he gradually and reluctantly admitted he had let his fear that I would provide stern competition for him prejudice his advice.

Another acquaintance later admitted he had been swept away with pleasure when I mentioned the project because he assumed that my asking his opinion was the initial step on my part to making him a partner in the new project.

A third, and even more surprising, reaction came from a man who revealed that he had downgraded the project because, some time before, the manufacturer whom my company was representing had sent him a *paltry Christmas gift.*

The experience taught me an interesting lesson. In seeking advice, you should go to people who are themselves in no way emotionally involved.

In another sense, the lesson goes even deeper than that. I know now that whenever I want advice about something I should try to gather as many opinions as I can, let all advice more or less sink in to an unconscious level, and then decide to make up my own mind regardless of what others have told me.

During your struggle for success, you have undoubtedly sought the opinions of many people close to you. And now that you are a fully established success, you might continue to consult those whose advice you know to be reasonably valid. But you must always return to your own particular intellectual analysis of the situation. Consider an important fact: if your past judgements hadn't been accurate, you wouldn't be where you are today.

Everyone you meet is prejudiced one way or another. The pessimist will find nothing good about what you have to tell him. The romanticist will imagine the most wildly idealistic results your project could produce. The man who is in the industry you hope to enter will undoubtedly consider you a potential competitor.

It's important to listen to what these people have to say. But if you are a truly successful individual, you yourself will supply the correct answers. Remember—*keep your eye on maintaining your success.* Aim towards a specific direction, and everything else will fall into line, including the right decisions.

And above all, when you want the advice of others, listen to everyone—but *do exactly what you yourself want to do.*

Success and Personal Happiness

One of the first rules we discussed in connexion with achieving the success goal was: *Don't overlook personal needs.* By the same token, once a person is successful, he has to make sure that he is supplied with a sufficient dosage of personal contentment. Otherwise, there's a strong chance success itself could slip through his fingers.

There's a very popular myth which seems to have been making the rounds of novels and films over the past twenty years or so: that the man who is an enormous success in his business or professional life has a miserable personal life. We're all familiar with the fictional character who stops at nothing to get ahead. We've watched or read about how he's clawed his way to the top and then, the moment he is in control of a virtual empire, he finds one of a number of things to be true: his wife hates him, or his children have turned against him, or else his friends have abandoned him. Though his professional power continues, he is, from a personal standpoint, a failure—a deeply lonely, basically unfulfilled man.

Frankly, I regard this current and all too popular theory as so much nonsense. If a man is *that* lonely or *that* unfulfilled, it's practically impossible for him to maintain the success he has. Personal happiness is one of the most necessary ingredients in the successful man's life. Often it's the very foundation upon which successful people build their entire careers.

I've seen cases, however, where a successful individual has been attacked by a personal tragedy which you would imagine would disrupt his success drive entirely. Once again, let me state that if the man is an authentic success, if his drive towards maintaining and enlarging upon his particular goal is that strong, he will somehow manage to override that tragedy. Not immediately, perhaps. But ultimately.

At times, the successful man may be knocked down, but not *out.*

Of course, the best thing you can do if you have a personal problem which is interfering in any way with your success is to rid yourself of it. Naturally, this isn't easy. Sometimes, it may involve ending a particular personal relationship which is plaguing you. Deeper problems might involve other approaches. But if there is a way (and you'll never know until you examine every possibility) to unload yourself of a dilemma that is in one way or another shackling you, you must pursue its solution until you're free once again to give your full attention to maintaining and possibly enlarging upon your success.

I know a man who, within a period of seven or eight years, rose to the top of his particular profession—the pharmaceutical industry. Then, quite suddenly, he announced to me he was leaving his wife and family for another woman. He had no intention of marrying the other woman, he told me. He simply could not see himself continuing to live with his wife while he carried on his extra-marital affair.

The months passed, and I detected enormous changes in him. He was drinking more than usual, and he had begun to neglect his business so much that it was really beginning to suffer. One day, this man came to me for advice. He was convinced his problem was a business problem and had almost completely disregarded in his own mind the possibility that his personal life was having a negative effect on his professional life.

I sensed at once what his problem was: he had always struck me as a family man, and I knew that it was *only in that particular role* that he could be fulfilled. I pointed this out to him. It was fairly clear to me that he had to do one of two things: either return to his wife and family, or marry the woman who was currently his mistress. To this man, the security of a strongly binding home life was an *absolute necessity*. I was sure that once he decided to do one of the two things I had suggested, his business life would return to normal.

Another important point to consider in maintaining personal happiness—every truly successful person I've met has a hobby which provides him with the true essence of that wonderful word "escapism". No matter how devoted we are to our careers, we all have to escape somewhere at some time in our daily lives, whether we do it by travelling to the Fiji Islands or by merely lying on our backs in our garages, tinkering with automobile parts.

Some people like to find hobbies entirely removed from their professions, so that the escapism is, in their eyes, complete. I for one like to find hobbies closely related to the field with which I'm concerned at the time. If I'm involved in theatrical productions, for example, I will make frequent trips to night clubs and theatres. If I am working on a new book, I will take great pleasure in meeting and conversing with people who I know will offer me a variety of backgrounds and points of view to help me with my writing.

Of course, if you can afford to travel—and nearly every successful person can—it is a necessity. Though travelling itself is bound to prove exciting, it is almost secondary to what happens to us in terms of our success. Invariably, we return to our jobs or professions so refreshed that we can come up with exciting new ways to contribute to our successes. Once again, by receiving pleasure in our personal lives, we are helping ourselves maintain the good fortunes of our professional accomplishments.

Success as a Way of Life

In any case, if you can turn your hobby into a large-scale area of excitement, at least 50 per cent of your personal life is bound to be fulfilling. As far as that other 50 per cent is concerned, remember you will always have problems of one sort or another. Try to do away with the ones that really interfere with your success. But if you can't, you must find a way to live with them. Otherwise, your success, one way or another, will be disrupted.

Remember, if you are determined to maintain your success, it is important to keep your personal life happy through whatever practical or philosophical approaches you feel will help you. In the long run, you will find that the more contentment you experience in your life, both in and away from your work, the more strongly solidified your success drives will be.

Success, Ethics and the Law

I feel since this book is primarily concerned with the way people determined to pursue or maintain success should behave, some mention has to be made concerning your attitude towards ethics and the law. Here again I'd like to attack a current myth.

We've already examined other bits and pieces of "success folklore". We've seen, for example, the true meaning of the word "luck". We've examined selfishness as it should be applied to our success goals, in a positive form. And in our previous category, I offered my opinion on the fictional character who is successful in his professional life but miserable from a personal standpoint.

Now I'd like to explode the theory that it is inevitable for the successful individual to be corrupt. Once again, as a fictional character, this type of individual offers us quite a bit of evil fascination in current films and novels. But is he authentic? I'd say, for the most part, he's not.

Remember, I am referring now—as throughout this section of the book—only to truly successful people. Not to the second-raters, too many of whom think that the art of getting ahead lies chiefly in drumming up a series of fantastic schemes to outwit others.

I would say, if we hope to maintain our success, it's an absolute necessity to carry with us a strong code of ethics. The fact that others in a field are behaving in an unethical manner is not a reason to act the same way.

Let me try to explain this. Compare the success competition to any field of sports. Think of the truly great champions. Were they great because they were unethical? In almost every case you will find that they were scrupulously ethical and still became champions.

This is my whole point. You will find a very strange thing occurring to you if you start being unethical. Somehow you will eventually end up with others who are doing the same things. Ultimately, their fate will become your fate. And there's always the chance that if you are among sharks another shark may bite you.

I've always believed the old axiom, when someone goes against the law in business, "It's more than a crime, it's a mistake."

I know of a rather curious incident which occurred several years ago and involved an enormously successful married couple, both of whom were working on the same account for an advertising agency. Within a very short period of time, the account had blossomed considerably until so much of the agency's attention was directed towards it that, if the account were to be lost, the agency itself would be in dire trouble.

As their careers progressed, the couple were respected by everyone in the industry. For one thing, they were both earning high salaries, and for another, their methods of making their particular product known to the public were enormously original and creative.

Apparently, however, the couple was dissatisfied with their lot in life and decided to embark on a scheme which they were convinced would bring them greater monetary rewards. They began by secretly peddling their account to other agencies, with the understanding that if another agency were to handle the account they would go along with the account to the new agency as account executives—only this time, not on a salary but a percentage basis, to receive a share of whatever profits the account brought the agency.

The secret peddling was so skilful a job of fancy manipulations—surreptitious meetings, private pacts drawn up between the client and the second agency—that the most adroit representative of Intelligence might have sat up and taken notice. Eventually, their scheme worked. The account fell directly into the hands of another agency. The couple moved comfortably into their new jobs, and their yearly income was increased considerably.

On the surface, it would seem that their unethical behaviour paid off. For a period of time, I suppose it did. But, as I've been stating all along, when we think in terms of our success, we must regard it in a broad sense, covering a period of years.

Let's examine the results of the advertising couple's actions.

When the initial agency lost the account, its billing dropped considerably. Many employees at the agency lost their jobs, and the head of the agency was forced into retirement. The story of the lost account and its disastrous

THE ANATOMY OF SUCCESS

results became common knowledge in the advertising industry. Trade journals printed a number of editorials about it, not mentioning the nefarious couple by name but hinting at who they were and at their scheme. Those really "in the know" in the advertising world were aware of the couple's identity.

Several years elapsed. Because of one of those inexplicable twists of fate that often occur in the business world, the corporation itself—the advertising couple's client—merged with another company. As a result, the account shifted to still a third agency, and the advertising couple lost their jobs.

Because of the deadly publicity they had received, the couple must have known what they were now in for: there wasn't a single large agency in the entire city which would dare hire the couple to handle an account of any significance. They were offered second-rate jobs, to be sure, but people at the larger agencies were aware of the lack of responsibility this couple had towards the agency for which they had once worked. The idea of granting them that kind of responsibility again seemed out of the question. Those in a hiring position were probably not even considering the ethics involved They were more likely simply *scared* of the couple.

Ultimately, the couple went to work for a third-rate advertising firm and have more or less faded into dismal obscurity.

Once again, the point I wish to make has little to do with moral considerations. I'm not offering a judgment on this couple for having "behaved badly". The only judgment I wish to make is that they made a *mistake*. Once you've established yourself as a person with a shaky code of ethics, others will know you for what you are. Sooner or later, those who are important are not going to trust you—and that lack of trust could result in your ruination.

Success as a Way of Life

Carrying out your business affairs in an illegal or un-ethical manner can on occasion produce results but in the long run, it is a difficult, unimaginative, and ultimately self-destructive means of handling your success.

Success and Reputation

Assume for a moment you are an inveterate boxing fan. One of your favourite fighters—a man you believe is one of those rare champions who have turned the game into an art—is scheduled to appear in your home city, and you hurry to buy yourself a ticket for the match. That evening, however, as you scan your local newspaper you happen to notice a news item informing you that the fighter staged a rowdy scene in an exclusive restaurant. The article also states in blunt terms that the man you idolize was drunk.

What do you do now? Does the article stir in you such negative feelings towards the fighter that you rush right back to the box office and ask for your money back? If you do, you're not like any of the boxing fans I happen to know.

Now, let's change the facts a little. You have some money you wish to invest, and a friend has recommended you visit a local banker whose advice, the friend assures you, is impec-cable. You telephone the banker's secretary and set up an appointment for the following morning. But that night, you happen to see an article in your local newspaper that the very man upon whose judgment you hope to rely was creating a drunken disturbance.

What is your reaction? You may decide to cancel the appointment entirely. Or if you do go to see this banker, you will certainly be looking at him with different eyes from what you might have, had you never read the article. In any case, chances are you will be prejudiced against him before the meeting, and you may be only too eager to dismiss any advice he has to offer you.

What has really happened in both these cases? Both men were drunk in appropriate places. Yet, only the second story upset you.

Logically speaking, if an individual is indiscreet enough to have become inebriated in a public place it shouldn't really have an effect on any advice he might offer concerning financial investments. What has really occurred, then, is that in the first case, the boxing champion's image has been altered very little. As far as you are concerned, what's an occasional fling with alcohol providing the boxer can really do his stuff in the ring? But in the second case, you feel a banker shouldn't behave that way. In short, his image has changed drastically.

Let's take another example that has to do with an individual's reputation: homosexuality. In some professions (the theatre and the fashion industry are prime examples), homosexuals are fully tolerated and their sexual and social behaviour accepted in a relatively relaxed manner on the part of heterosexuals. I know one married couple in the textile industry, for instance, whose wide range of friends and business acquaintances include a number of confirmed male homosexuals. Without any amount of forced sophistication on their part, the married couple make sure to invite these homosexuals with their current boy friends to a party in the same way you would invite young ladies and ask them to bring along their escorts.

But try to imagine a similar situation among a group of people in, for example, the teaching profession—or, even more absurd, in political circles.

The facts are very clear. We must always take into account the field in which we are working when we decide what sort of personal reputations we must exhibit before others. If you are a bank president, it is professional suicide to become a gambler of any proportions. On the other hand, if you are the head of a union, you can embark on violent quarrels with the U.S. government and be hated by the public as long as you *protect your union*. A motion-picture actress can be named as co-respondent in a divorce case and happily discover the publicity has started her career soaring to unlimited possibilities. But just imagine what would happen to a prominent female surgeon, given similar publicity.

Whether your reputation is "moral" or "immoral", "profligate" or "virtuous" matters only in relation to your success and to the field in which it is achieved. Your "behaviour" is only important in the context of maintaining this success. All other considerations are not part of the anatomy of success.

Conclusion

7 The Most Important Ingredient: Experience

I KNOW A WOMAN WHO, FOR THE PAST TEN YEARS OR SO, has been determined to go on a diet. When she initially made up her mind to take this step, she weighed close to one hundred and seventy pounds.

Only recently, I was invited to a dinner party at this friend's home and discovered much to my amusement that, over the past ten years, she had built up the most definitive collection of books on dieting that I've ever seen. Her bookshelves were fairly bursting with an extraordinary array of elaborate and expensive volumes on how to lose weight. Acquiring such a collection might have been considered admirable had this been my friend's primary intention. But I regret to report that her sole purpose had been merely to lose weight. And at her dinner party, she sadly informed me that she still weighed close to one hundred and seventy pounds. She added that she read every book, but never applied any of the methods described.

Acquiring success is, in some ways, like dieting. You must apply the formulae and principles to *experience itself* in order to see results.

We have examined the steps we have to take in order to become successful. We have seen how important it is to maintain our achievements by exploring ways to behave, and by investigating the relationship between ourselves and our success.

We've viewed the facts. We've studied the rules. Now we must go out into whatever area we happen to choose and apply those rules to *practical experience*.

Essentially, if we are to assure our lasting success, we will be covering seven basic steps:
1. Analyse yourself.
2. Choose your field.
3. Analyse the field you have chosen.
4. Choose your goal within that field.
5. Prepare your plan to achieve the chosen goals.
6. Execute your plan.
7. Protect your achievements.

As we move from step to step, cautiously and a trifle uncertain in the beginning, our strength will grow.

Remember: the world of success is open to everyone. Clear your minds of the mythological aura which seems to surround success and successful individuals. Once you do that, the occasional failure you may experience will have very little effect on your over-all battle strategy. Before very long, you'll see how easy it is to make the number of failures diminish and to increase your positive gains.

Experience itself is the most important ingredient in the anatomy of success.